Contents

Text Stories

TOTAL ECLIPSE OF THE HEART............5
Written by Oli Smith. Illustrations by Martin Geraghty.

THE END OF THE RAINBOW..............15
Written by Jacqueline Rayner. Illustrations by Brian Williamson.

SCARED STIFF..............................24
Written by Mark Gatiss. Illustrations by Ben Willsher.

BENNELONG POINT........................41
Written by Keith Temple. Illustrations by Neill Cameron.

THE SHAPE ON THE CHAIR...............50
Written by Matt Jones. Illustrations by David A Roach.

KNOCK KNOCK!............................58
Written by Paul Magrs. Illustrations by Adrian Salmon.

THE HALDENMOR FUGUE.................68
Written by James Moran. Illustrations by Andy Walker.

Comic Strip

SPACE VIKINGS!...........................33
Written by Jonathan Morris. Art by Rob Davis & Ian Culbard.

Afterword

A LETTER FROM THE DOCTOR.........77
Forwarded to us by Russell T Davies.

EDITOR & DESIGNER **CLAYTON HICKMAN**

FRONT COVER PAINTING BY **ALISTER PEARSON**

FRONTISPIECE ILLUSTRATION BY **ANDY WALKER** CONTENTS PAGE ILLUSTRATION BY **BEN WILLSHER**

WITH SPECIAL THANKS TO **RUSSELL T DAVIES, GARY RUSSELL, TOM SPILSBURY, PERI GODBOLD, SCOTT GRAY, PETER WARE, DAVID TURBITT** & ALL AT BBC WORLDWIDE

DEDICATED TO **DAVID TENNANT** WITH LOVE AND THANKS

Total Eclipse of The Heart

WRITTEN BY **OLI SMITH**   ILLUSTRATIONS BY **MARTIN GERAGHTY**

t was six hours until total eclipse over Houston as the *Heart* pirouetted out of Earth's orbit, catching the last dying embers of the sun.

The starship spun into its slingshot trajectory against the moon, yellow rings from the stabiliser rockets rippling across its body, shots of blue from the ion engines adjusting velocity until, after thirty minutes, its shadow was racing across the white lunar dawn below. Plugs slotted silently into place and the bullet blossomed into a golden flower of solar sails.

Then the engine room exploded.

'You are kidding me. You have *got* to be kidding me!' Arnold slammed his hand against the screen. 'This is what you get for outsourcing. Who the hell thought China could handle ion engines? Seriously, Captain, you?'

'Who the hell thought you could talk so much? When you've quite finished Arnold, I've got Mission Control waiting to be patched through.'

Arnold withered into a sulk.

'Apologies, Captain.' He rolled his eyes. 'But I can't wait to see their response to this. Priceless.'

Mission Control fizzed onto the main screen.

'Captain Jacobs.' The grey-haired, grey-faced controller on the screen acknowledged the ship's commander. 'The boys here are doing the math as we speak. Seems like you've still got three engines from the readouts, shouldn't be too much of a problem – what does your engineer say?'

Jacobs gave Arnold a sidelong glance. 'Our engineer doesn't seem to have anything constructive to add at this point in time, sir. But I think Elena's been running diagnostics.'

Elena was the perfect professional, but Arnold was sure he saw a smirk tickle the corner of her lips as she looked across at him. He pointedly averted his gaze back to the view screen as she spoke.

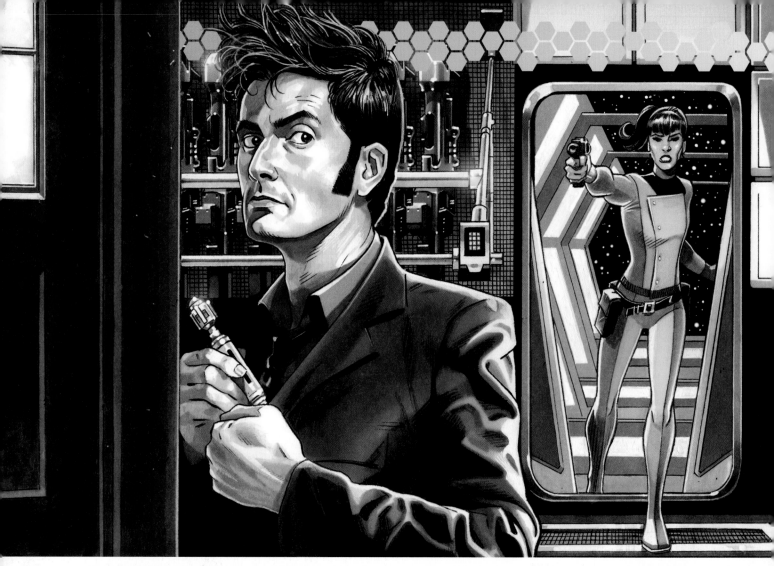

'We've lost pressure to the engine room so I've had to seal it off. Which does mean a spacewalk for emergency repairs if we want to stay on schedule. I'd also like to point out that we are having trouble compensating our trajectory due to the power requirements at this time.'

The Controller looked down at a sheaf of papers just handed to him by a nervous man from the desk behind. 'Okay, thank you Elena. The results here indicate a lucky escape for you guys – the damage looks repairable, I'm sending the schematics over to you now. We suggest you get out there ASAP. An investigation into the structural integrity of the hyperdrive is also recommended. Just to make sure.'

'Confirmed sir.'

'Oh, one last thing Jacobs.' He squinted at his papers once more. 'You've got a mass anomaly down in small-arms. Might want to check it out.'

The Doctor grinned as his sonic screwdriver whirred across the rows of pistols and rifles that stretched from floor to ceiling, the TARDIS neatly parked between the shelves behind him. He bobbed his head in time to the tinkling rhythm of bullets falling at his feet as each casing dismantled itself in a shower of screws. Deftly, he caught one and cracked it open, sniffing the tiny mound of powder inside.

'Two thousand and seventy... something. Fantastic! The beginning of the Unified Earth. Which means I can get a decent cup of tea, a custard cream and a good book anywhere I fancy. Shame about the chips though, I never really enjoyed fries, not greasy enough for me. I love greasy chips. And vinegar, lots of vinegar.' The Doctor's face fell with the realisation that there was nobody there to listen to him. He scowled at the TARDIS. 'You completely count, you know. Don't give me that look.'

He hadn't noticed the soft hiss of hydraulics behind him, as the heavy metal door slid open, revealing the silhouette of a young woman, standing not-quite-confidently, in the frame.

'Excuse me. Would you mind giving me one good reason why I shouldn't shoot you right now?' she said.

The Doctor didn't blink.

'See? She was probably there the whole time. So I *definitely* wasn't talking to myself.' He turned to face the jump-suited figure with a beaming smile, hands patting his pockets a little too expertly for Danielle's liking. 'Ah, hello! Sorry I haven't said 'hi' as yet, a bit of trouble adjusting to your gravity – centrifugal, yes? Anyway that's all sorted now because I've got my pass right here. The Doctor, UNIT.' He thrust the psychic paper at her so eagerly it almost slapped her nose.

The smooth titanium of the hull arced gracefully in all directions, enhanced by the gleaming white letters sprayed across the side of the ship, each one half a mile high. *HEART*.

Column Two marked the halfway point from the airlock to the engines, and the suited figures paused to take in the golden reflections of the sun, mirrored a thousand times in the precisely mapped mathematical contours of the sails. Captain Jacobs raised a thickly padded hand to shield the glare that stung his eyes, even through the tinted visor.

'You have to admit, it's gorgeous.' He tilted his head to Elena in search of some similar appreciation. She nodded acknowledgement but displayed no emotion.

Arnold's voice crackled over the radio.

'Lets do the admiring when it's a new sun in the sky please, guys. We've got work to do.'

'Well why don't you come down and do this then?' Elena snapped. 'A bit of hard work might help you get over that foul mood of yours. It's not like you haven't done it before.'

The engineer snorted. 'I would if I could, but sadly you monkeys haven't spent the last four years learning the coding techniques to recalibrate the engines from here, so unless you'd rather take a sudden vacation on the moon the moment you fire them back up,

I don't really have a choice. Hell, you wouldn't even recognise half the symbols I'm looking at right now. I'm up here because I know the language of something complex and beautiful and you're down there because you have a degree in social science.'

'But mainly,' Elena hissed, 'because you're in a mood. Anyway I did bioengineering; it was Danielle that did social science.'

'And she's running round the ship to check the storerooms. Fat lot of good she is.'

'Shut up, you two,' Jacobs cut in. 'We're getting the job done now, and by the time we get back I want a serious attitude change up there Arnold. You get me?'

'I get you, I get you. But this stuff should have been checked before we left. Didn't anyone care if it worked? We're travelling further than ninety percent of the people back home can understand, but our engines can't even take us into slingshot without blowing up!'

'As long as they get us into the right position to engage the hyper-drive in four hours then I don't care what they do,' Jacobs sighed. 'This mission cannot fail. Do you really want to go back to an Earth without the *Heart* project? Do you remember what it was like?'

'I understand that,' Arnold muttered. 'I just wish it didn't have such a girly name...'

'Don't get me wrong, Danielle. I like quiet people. They listen. They pick up on a lot of things most people would miss. But we've been walking for ages and you haven't said a word.' Even the Doctor's long legs were having difficulty matching the pace of the woman hurrying ahead of him down the ribbed grey corridors of the ship. 'Let's slow down, have a chat, take the scenic route, all that stuff. We've got a few hours before the eclipse yet.'

He straightened his tie and grinned a grin. 'Which reminds me, is there anywhere we can get a good view? That's what I'm here for really. This one's meant to be beautiful.'

Danielle frowned. 'A good view? I don't know what they said to you in the briefing, but once the eclipse is directly over Houston we'll only have about a minute before the hyperdrive engages and the ship dematerialises. Twenty-six light years in six hours – can you believe it? A new home. A new start. A new Earth. Centauri-Beta.'

The Doctor tripped on a rib, slapped his palm on the wall to regain balance and quickly ran a hand through his hair as if nothing had happened.

'Hold on a second, this is a colony ship? Now I'm sure that's a stupid question – but when you've just spent half an hour in a room full of guns you get a little sceptical.'

'A precaution.' Her voice was haughty. 'We'll be creating a society out of newborns; you must have some enforcement to authority if you want to create a civilisation from scratch. There will be no link to Earth once we make planetfall, of course. It's too far away. Anyway, it's not *a* colony ship, it's *the* colony ship. *The Heart of Planet Earth* – the reason the war is over. Through this ship we are united in our goal to start again. Have you people really specialised so much you forgot why you built the hyperdrive?'

'No no no, this isn't right, this is twenty-seventy something.' The Doctor screwed his face up; trying to remember a timeline he only experienced at random intervals. 'Hyperdrive thingies are way off – after Mars, Europa and those other colonies. Are you sure?'

She stopped suddenly and stared at the Doctor as if he was an idiot. 'Of *course* I'm sure. You people and NASA had been sitting on the technology for years waiting for a safe window to reveal it. Boy did you time *that* right.' She paused in the corridor. 'I say "you people", but actually I don't think you are with UNIT, are you, Doctor?'

The Doctor winked. 'Ah, but my piece of paper says I am. And that's what really matters in the end, isn't it?' He paused. 'Does that worry you?'

'Not really. Too much money's gone into this project for Houston to bring it down. You've nowhere to run if you are a terrorist and if you aren't it looks like you'll be the fifth human to step onto an alien planet. I hope you're properly excited.'

'Very!' The Doctor beamed and darted ahead down the corridor. 'Now, can I have a look at these newborns? I'm fascinated about how you plan to populate a planet with only four people.'

* ◆ *

'Houston reports radio blackout in two, Captain. The hyperdrive is on standby until remote contact is re-established. Radiation levels in the engine room should be at a minimum. You have three hours before we round the moon to complete repairs – I suggest you get a move on.'

'Received Arnold. Approaching the damage now.' Jacobs hit the switch to dim his visor. Above him the brilliant white of the lunar surface spun, dizzyingly quickly, as the ship hurtled on its course. His magnetic boots skidded on the hull as it twisted away in front of him, an ugly gash in an otherwise polished skin.

Elena was already inside, falling upside-down to Jacobs' point of view as the interior gravity reoriented her.

Despite the carefully regulated atmosphere inside the helmet, it still felt colder in the dark of the engine room compared to the glare of the ship's hull.

'It's strange,' said the captain. 'I thought it was a meteorite that hit us.'

'There was always a slight probability of that occurring. We just got unlucky I guess. Those things travel so fast they could puncture a hole in anything.' Elena was too busy wresting panels away from

the tangled cables which fed into the cavernous blackness above to indulge Jacobs' musings.

'But if a meteorite really did hit us, surely the hull should be bent *inwards*?'

Elena froze, then looked up at the captain with horror.

* ◆ *

'You aren't listening,' Danielle said, halting mid explanation.

The Doctor was striding around the circular floor of the birthing chamber, head held high, arms outstretched.

'Homo sapiens! Indomitable! Sitting here amongst the stars, blah blah, that sort of thing.' He jammed his hands into his coat pockets. 'You know, it's a lot harder to say things like that when all you're talking to is a bunch of test tubes.'

He leaned in to inspect the small glass capsules that spiralled around the warm white walls of the room, three storeys high. 'Anyway, I *was* listening. So far you'd got to the bit where you'd all realised that this Great War was destroying the planet, decided to call a ceasefire, and invested your respective countries' communal incomes in the *Heart* project as a demonstration of the Earth's desire to start anew. It was quite moving, actually.'

Danielle looked a little put out, but carried on regardless. 'So that no one country could claim ownership of the craft itself, every country contributed a component proportional to their investment. From the solar sails down to the chairs. The work of one hundred and ninety-four nations is all around you. And regardless of their respective wealth or size, they each donated–'

'One hundred samples of genetic material. I can tell from the labelling. Very nice.' The Doctor tilted his head, numbers whizzing through his mind. 'The combinations you could create from a couple of tens of thousands of different genes would be... well, very big. Too big for you to have to worry about inbreeding anyway.'

Danielle tapped a code into a wall panel near the door and the Doctor had to hop to one side as a circular section of floor rose with a hiss and a gasp of steam. Four glass tanks, clustered together, rose with it. Suspended in each one was a semi-formed human embryo, the umbilical cord snaking into a central nutrient pipe.

'We have nearly five hundred of these blank embryos ready for fertilisation upon arrival.' The Doctor was already on his knees, nose pressed against the glass, waving his sonic screwdriver over the white tissue inside. 'When each reaches a week's maturity,' Danielle went on, 'various genetic combinations will be implanted into the foetuses to create new, unique people. Newborns.'

She put her hands on her hips, and motherly pride showed on her face.

'And this works? For sure? You've seen it happen?'

'Well, of course it works!' Danielle's face became frosty again. The thought that it might not work had never even occurred to her. 'I mean I haven't seen it *personally*, but the technology's cutting edge. Why wouldn't it work? Besides, it's mostly automated. I don't really come in until the first generation is born. I'm in charge of the breeding plans and initial societal structures mostly.'

'And that's your job? Nanny?'

Danielle sighed. 'My job, Doctor, is to make sure everybody gets along swimmingly.'

The Doctor flashed her a smile. 'I hope the pay's good!'

Manual work in low gravity was always tedious. Nothing felt quite as it should, every touch was exaggerated. Cables twisted and careened around Jacobs as he worked, looming at him unnervingly through the shadows. He stripped his section and applied the coupling, then he scrambled upright and touched his radio.

'Elena? Are you finished with the regulators up there? I'm ready to re-engage the remote ignition.' Her reply was faded by distance and radiation.

'I have to reinstall the box and apply the limiters, then we're go.'

'Confirmed.'

The captain waited patiently in the dark, hands on the crank that would screw the giant conductors together. The radio buzzed and through a shrill crackle of static he heard Arnold's voice, the word 'engage.'

Obediently he turned the wheel.

'Wait wait, do not engage, I repeat *do not* engage, I've missed something. There's a fluid link needs repressurising, the whole system's hot.' Arnold's voice was shattered by a burst of static fuzz. Jacobs tried to jerk his head away from the earpiece but couldn't. 'How could I have missed this? Oh my God you have to get out of there! Capt–' The speaker tore and the Captain was deaf. He reeled in pain.

The air above him crackled. Flashes reflected in his visor, dazzling Jacobs as his head turned upwards.

Showers of sparks were arcing over his head from the other side of the skyscraper engine, bouncing off the walls.

Brief flashes of clarity in the emptiness. Pipes, rods, cogs. Elena.

He had to half-close his eyes to make her out at first, tripping and stumbling down the inside curve of the hull toward him, upside down. He saw her twisting and reeling in painful slow motion as she fell. Jacobs' jaw dropped as he realised what he'd done.

Blindly he felt for the crank, gloves slipping on the handle.

But it was too late.

The ion engine jump-started.

The last thing he saw before the blue energy burnt him away was Elena's body, reduced to ash, settling on his visor.

The Doctor hurled himself into the control room in a blur of suit and sideburns. Instinctively adjusting dials and levers, he tried desperately to compensate the wildly spinning trajectory of the ship.

'Come on come on come on, hold still!' he hissed through gritted teeth.

Danielle rushed past him to the hunched figure of a body heaving in the strobing red alarm light. She grabbed him by the shoulders and slapped him.

'What happened? Tell me what happened! Report!'

'They're gone, vaporised. Oh God, it's my fault. Oh God. They're dead Danni, completely dead.' His voice grated to a hoarse whisper. 'I wanted to save them. I could have saved them.'

Through the tears Arnold automatically thumbed the cooling switches in time to the Doctor's adjustments, confirming checks and shifting balances. Danielle was thrown backwards against the wall as the ship strained to keep pace with the conflicting coordinates it was being fed.

Still on autopilot, Arnold fired up the three intact ion engines, straightening the craft, so the Doctor could reset the orbit without the need to overcompensate.

On the display, the angry peaks slowed into a curving line.

The shuddering ceased and the alarms quietened.

Arnold seemed to forget he was crying and smeared his face with his sleeve. Blinking, he looked across the room. He saw the Doctor jamming his screwdriver into the ship's hard drive. His hand moved to his hip and the pistol holstered there.

'It's okay, he's UNIT,' Danielle said, stepping between them. 'Stowed on board to make sure things ran smoothly.'

'Well they haven't, have they?' Arnold's voice was strained, high-pitched. 'He can abort the damn mission. Take us home. He'll have the authority.'

'I'm sorry Arnold, I'm sure we all want to go home, but right now it doesn't look like we're going to get that luxury.' The Doctor was squinting at the sonic screwdriver. He ran his fingers through his hair and looked up. 'I'll show you, give me one second.' He slammed the control panel with his fist. 'If I can just bounce the signal off an outlying satellite, direct it around the moon, we should... ah! Here you go.'

He looked up at the viewscreen as it flickered into life.

'It's the news,' Danielle said. 'Israeli, by the looks of it.'

'Exactly,' said the Doctor, grim-faced. 'But what's bad, what's really, *really* bad, is that there's no news but good news.'

◇ ◆ ◇

'It was hard, very hard to spot. A beautiful piece of deception.

Accurate in almost every detail. Almost. But it was the birthing room which gave away that something wasn't quite right. I mean, *technically*, it should work. The theory's sound. But what you have in those tanks are mindless drones and nothing more. The embryos are too fully formed by the time you implant the genetic combinations for them to have any effect. Plus, with no acceleration at the growth stage, how many babies do you think will survive to adulthood with just four crew members to look after them? Completely impractical, and the people who installed it must have known – they were just told to shut up. When every single part is made in a different country, it wouldn't be too hard for a couple of them to have their corners cut without anybody noticing.'

Danielle had listened to the Doctor's speech without a flicker of emotion. 'But if that's true, and the whole mission was never meant to succeed, what...' her voice cracked slightly. 'What in God's name is supposed to happen to us?'

The Doctor rubbed his chin. 'To answer that, I think I'll have to pass you over to Arnold here – as I'm afraid he's holding a gun to my head.' He stepped aside and Arnold's gun arm followed him, straight and unwaveringly confident.

He cocked the pistol – the click echoing round the silent control room.

'Not another word, Doctor,' he hissed. 'We've lost too many people already for you to condemn her to death as well.'

◇ ◆ ◇

The hull was in shadow, the sun setting over the horizon of the moon, defining every crater, rims burning white. Not long to go now. The solar sails creaked silently as they folded in on themselves. Their purpose fulfilled, they eased into the body of the ship, oblivious to the two suited figures picking their way over the metal struts on their way to the engine room.

The Doctor didn't have time to admire the view.

'How long had you known?'

'I'm the engineer Doctor, the first thing I did before boarding was take the engines apart and put them back together. Come on,

did you really think UNIT could sit on something as major as hyperdrive technology? They're inept at the best of times. You scientists think you're so damn clever – that the rest of us will just accept anything you say as the truth, assuming it's too complicated for our simple little minds to comprehend.'

'Arnold, just tell me what the hyperdrive actually is. You've probably guessed that I'm not associated with UNIT by now. Well, not at the moment anyway. I'm not here to help with a cover-up. I'm a sightseer, just passing through. I want to help.'

Arnold gave a short laugh. 'It's a firework, Doctor. That's all. When Houston triangulates the jump they'll send through a radio signal that will ignite the whole ship, a rainbow of flame running along its length, burning it to nothing. To the people watching on Earth it'll look like the hyperdrive's engaged, I mean they've never seen one before, what else would it look like? To them the difference between dematerialisation and disintegration is how a NASA official on TV defines it. He'll tell them we've travelled light-years in seconds, so far away that it will take decades before they could receive any transmission we send. And in thirty years, when those transmissions don't arrive, it won't matter – the mission will have served its purpose. Unified the Earth, taking our civilisation on to bigger and better things. Who'd remember a tiny colony ship when their home world is such a paradise?'

The Doctor ducked under a semi-folded girder. The structural damage in this area meant that full retraction of the sails was impossible. Arnold followed, pushing the sail material aside. It was brittle, and splintered into shards of gold leaf. Affected by the gravity of the interior, it followed the astronauts down into the engine room, falling softly onto the floor.

'So why didn't you tell them? Why didn't you tell your crewmates you were all going to die?'

Arnold turned and flicked his visor tint off. Their helmets almost touched, and the Doctor could see the fire behind his eyes.

'Because I believed in it. It was the right thing to do. We needed the *Heart* project so badly. That was why I still boarded this ship, in spite of what I knew. That was why I sabotaged the engine room.'

The Doctor's eyebrows arched, visible even in the darkness.

'Don't you see Doctor? If I'd told them, we'd *all* have been dead by now. It would have been too big a risk for NASA to keep us alive with that knowledge. Best to keep it a secret, damage the mission another way – something unrelated to the hyperdrive. That way we could abort the mission in innocence. We'd survive and the project would still have had its effect. God, how naïve does that sound now?' A tear formed in his eye. The Doctor shrugged and set his jaw.

'People aren't machines, Arnold. You can't use logic to predict what a society on the verge of self destruction will resort to.'

'Then Jacobs and Elena died and I don't even know why, I shouldn't have missed that leak. I'm so scared Doctor, what if I did it deliberately? What if somewhere, subconsciously, I ignored the readings to save my own skin, to stop the engines coming back online?'

Fists clenched, his body contorted in anguish.

'And you told Danni! We can't go back now, none of us – you've seen the news, no-one knows what's happening up here. They're never going to abort, whatever we do!'

Danielle angrily ripped off the patronising note Arnold had stuck to the monitor before he'd left: *Don't. Touch. Anything!!!*

She swore and slumped in the pilot's chair.

There was a sudden burst of static and the screen crackled and shifted into clarity once more. The faded face of Mission Control mouthed silently for a second before the sound kicked in.

'–cobs? Are you receiving me? Captain Jacobs? We have radio

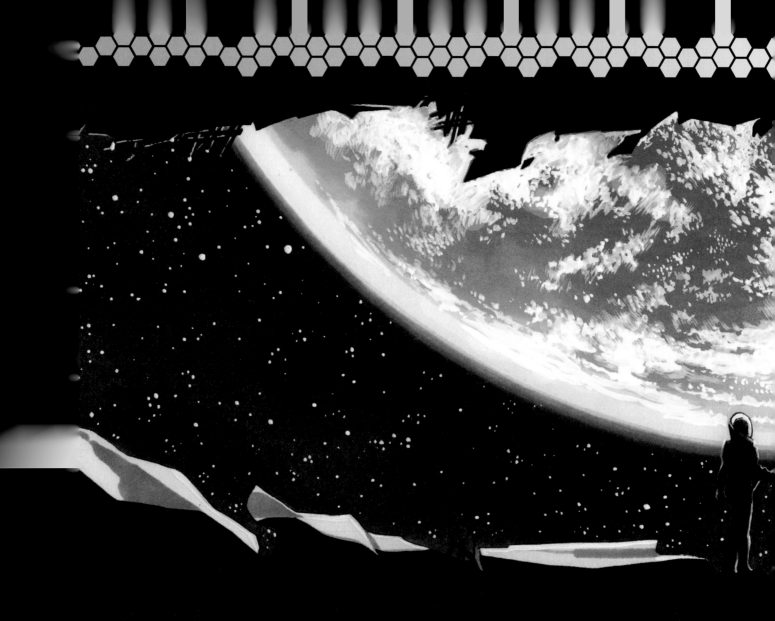

contact re-established. Only half an hour to jump, maintain current trajectory. Captain Jacobs, please confirm.'

Danielle's breath came heavily, and her palms began to sweat as she moved her hand above the switch that could accept or cut off the transmission. Finally, she flicked a switch and stood up. Mission Control received visual and the controller blinked in surprise.

'Danielle?'

'Captain Jacobs is dead, sir.' Danielle's voice dripped venom. 'And in half an hour the rest of us will be too.'

The picture shifted slightly, a sign that the channel had been switched to an encoded frequency. The controller shuffled some papers and looked at the floor and then the ceiling.

'I'm sorry, Danielle. There is a problem with the signal, we didn't get that. Cycling alternative frequencies.'

'I know you can hear me!' Her voice became a shout. 'You set us up, there's no Centauri-Beta, and even if there is we aren't going there.'

The controller bit his pen and muttered something under his breath.

'Acknowledge me!' Danielle screamed.

'It doesn't look like we can get you back guys, visual or audio. Only a minor fault though – the eclipse is directly overhead, our astronomers have confirmed accurate sightings on the star system from both observatories.'

Danielle tugged at her hair. 'I don't care!'

The controller calmly continued. 'We are compensating for the sun's gravity which will no doubt throw us off somewhat, but without the sunlight obscuring visual contact with the second

triangulation location, we should be able to get you to within a half light-year of the planet. You have three minutes. Your hyperdrive should be cooling down now. I suggest you strap yourselves in, there's likely to be some turbulence from the spatial displacement ripple, just remember you're in safe hands.'

With a yell of frustration, Danielle slammed her fist into the image of the controller's face and felt it crack satisfyingly. But the picture still held.

He turned to focus on her then, his slate eyes connecting with her blue. Though her own sight was blurred by tears, she could still see his eyes watering.

'I don't know if you can hear me up there, guys. I hope you can, because...' He removed his glasses and wiped them with his tie. 'Because I just want to say. From all of us down here. That you've given us hope. Hope for a real future, a better future. I wish you luck in your new life, from the bottom of my heart, and I hope that, when you get to your utopia, when you look up at the stars with their strange and wonderful new constellations, you'll think of us on this tiny blue planet, millions of miles away, trying, like you, to start a new life.'

He stifled a choke. 'Because we can't go back, Danni, we can't. Houston out.'

The massive bulk of the ion engine dwarfed the Doctor and Arnold as they crawled along it, picking through tubes and wreckage, searching for connectors and switches, broken panels and sparking joints. The engine room was so big they could barely make out the

shadows of the adjacent rockets, let alone the coiling screw of what they had supposed to be the hyperdrive. The brief flares of both the sonic screwdriver and Arnold's blowtorch were the only lights in the suffocating blackness. But Arnold still fingered his gun.

'Why are we doing this? We're wasting time.' The Doctor's voice came over the helmet radio. 'I've got a ship, I can take you away from here now, before it's too late.'

Arnold turned to him. 'I believe you, I really do. But we can't go – I owe it to Elena, and Jacobs. They can't die for nothing, not because of me.'

The Doctor was nonplussed. 'But why does it matter if we fix the engine? The ship will explode anyway, so what if it's in a slightly different position?'

Arnold smacked his panel down and welded it shut. 'It matters because down there, on Earth, everybody, and I mean *everybody*, is watching us. Not just Mission Control, but kids with their dad's telescope, conspiracy nerds in their sheds, journalists, governments, the whole wide stupid world. And if *anybody*, for one second, spots that the ship is facing the wrong way, then imagine the inquiries that will follow. The arguments, the violence. We can't afford to start the blame game after we have invested everything in this mission. Hell, they even timed the mission with the eclipse so we could apparently triangulate the trajectory better without the sun getting in the way. For all I know, they probably have a working route to Centauri-Beta ready for when we finally, actually, invent a hyperdrive.' He stopped, and tried to wipe the sweat from his brow, then remembered the helmet. 'Although if you want to know what I really think, I think we tied it in with an eclipse so that everyone down there

gets the greatest pyrotechnical show of their lives. I suppose that's worth something.'

Silently, the Doctor pocketed the screwdriver, and pushed himself towards Arnold. He rotated himself into a standing position and held out his gloved hand to the crouching engineer. He took it.

The light of the Earth edged into the engine room as the two men shook hands. The Doctor turned his visor into the faded dawn.

'Now that's beautiful,' he said.

Like the pupil of an eye, deep blue, flecked with white, the planet dawned through the tear in the hull.

With a roar, the hyperdrive coil shuddered into life, the whole ship vibrating as it began to rotate, slowly at first, but gathering speed.

'No, no, no! We're too late!' Arnold's voice was stuttering over the radio, the signal drenched with interference. 'Doctor, you have to get back to the cockpit, we haven't got much time. I'll read you out the coordinates when you get there. You have to programme them in, set the engines on standby. Take Danni and get out of here. Go!'

The Doctor was struggling to stay upright, his grip unsteady.

'But what about you?'

'I have to finish here, get the engine back online. The computer will take over once that's done. I can do it. Save Danni, there's no point us all dying.'

The Doctor felt a sharp pain in his chest, a pistol jammed into his space-suit, pushing him away.

The Doctor had to shout to make himself heard now. 'I'm not going to let you do this, Arnold. It doesn't have to end this way!'

Arnold's reply was lost in static. But the gun in his hand was steady. He'd made his choice. He pointed it at the Doctor. Gestured toward the hole in the hull.

The Doctor took a step back and paused. As the coil above them began to glow, he looked into the frightened face of the engineer, and saw his lips mouth one word.

'Run!'

So he did.

The *Heart* rounded the dark side of the moon, a streamlined silver bullet once again.

It skimmed out of the satellite's gravity, drifting into alignment – its nose pointing outwards, beyond the sun. The ion engines ignited, a burst of blue light illuminating the craters below as the ship picked up speed, racing toward the sunrise and silhouetted against the eclipse.

Finally, before the first rays of the corona could reach around and swallow the tiny speck of metal in their golden hue, the hyperdrive engaged.

It spun the ship like a bullet – faster and faster until, just for a second, a new sun blossomed.

Green, blue, yellow, red cascades of light. An infinite chain of explosions shimmered along the length of the ship, fading into flames, then sparks, then glimmers of light, then nothing.

The *Heart* was gone, and the Earth cheered.

In Houston, as his colleagues crowded round and plied him with champagne, the controller announced his retirement.

He slid his jacket from the back of his chair and walked calmly from the room, closed the door to the sounds of applause, rested his head against the wall.

'I'm sorry,' he said, and called his wife.

Pink skies reflected a rosy glow onto the rolling hills of Centauri-Beta. The atmosphere was cool, still and refreshing. Condensation gathered around the mugs as the Doctor chinked a tiny spoon around the insides. He perched a single custard cream carefully inside each handle and reached across to place one of the mugs on the arm of the deckchair next to him, the one with the faded picture of a Care Bear. It was on its last legs, but he liked to keep the 'Best Dad in the World' one for himself.

Danielle took a sip of tea and shivered, the warmth of the drink reminding her how cold the air was here. She moved her hand through the rising heat above the cup, and sighed.

'Not quite a new Earth, I know,' said the Doctor. 'But destinations don't get much better than this one. Those scientists knew their stuff after all.'

Danielle stretched her legs, then carefully rose from the chair. 'If you don't mind, Doctor, I think I'll take a walk. I want to see the view from the top of the hill.'

'Be my guest. Best not go too far though, the grass pheromones get a bit intoxicating at high altitudes. It's almost *too* beautiful.'

He watched Danielle as she walked away, her head held high, her body strong, a tear in her eye – blue flecked with white.

Leaning back in his chair he pushed his damp fringe from his eyes and squinted at the stars, shimmering through the rose-coloured sky. Constellations unfamiliar and wonderful.

The tea was already cold when he remembered to drink again.

THE END

The End of the Rainbow

WRITTEN BY **JACQUELINE RAYNER** ILLUSTRATIONS BY **BRIAN WILLIAMSON**

The cat rubbed itself happily against the Doctor's legs then, in the fickle way of felines, wandered off without a backward glance in search of newer and better entertainments.

Because the extraordinary was everyday for the Doctor, it took him quite five seconds to realise that there was something very odd about the cat – at least, assuming he really had landed in a small English town near the beginning of the twenty-first century, because cats in small English towns near the beginning of the twenty-first century tended not to be coloured bright green.

There could be a reasonable – and dull – explanation for this phenomenon, of course; mischievous children and pots of dye sprang to mind. But the Doctor held out his hopes for something a

bit more interesting as he jogged off after the cat, and it soon looked as though his optimism would be rewarded. Sounds were drifting on the air towards him as he neared the high street: shouts and exclamations and cries, laughter that sounded amused and laughter that sounded close to hysterics.

People were coming out of buildings to see what was happening, and some of them looked up and cried out too. The Doctor, seeing this, also glanced upwards. And stopped in amazement.

It was beautiful; utterly, wonderfully beautiful. But it was also incredible, and quite, quite impossible. There above them all was a rainbow. Not a far away refraction of light in the sky but a curve of colour that sliced through the air and came down to earth – as the Doctor was soon to discover – just outside a greengrocer's shop.

The shouting, crying and laughing crowd was clustered round the shop, but the Doctor's air of authority carried him through to the front. And there was the end of the rainbow, slap bang in the middle of some trays of fruit. The display, artfully arranged to tempt buyers inside the shop, now seemed to contain the bizarrest tropical fare: violet apples, blue bananas and indigo pears. To create the maximum confusion, even the oranges had changed colour, no longer orange but brilliant scarlet red.

A tall man with a moustache and a striped apron was trying to shield the rainbow, flinging his arms as wide as they would go to make a barrier. 'Don't touch it, don't touch it!' he was saying, but the people in the crowd were held back only by their own nervousness, not his words. Nevertheless they pushed forwards, not wanting to risk missing anything. Suddenly a surge from behind sent those at the front stumbling forwards. The Doctor kept his footing, but the old woman who'd been standing next to him fell, her outstretched arms brushing across the inside of the rainbow.

The Doctor helped her to her feet. 'It's all right, I'm a doctor – well, sort of – anyway, it's all right...'

But she wasn't listening to him. She began to whimper in fear and horror. Her hands, still held out in front of her, were gradually turning violet. The fingertips first, then over the knuckles and down to the palms, then the colour was spreading across the wrists and up the arms, like blotting paper dipped in ink.

'Oh crikey, another one,' moaned the aproned man. 'Won't listen to me, will they? Keep trying to tell 'em... Come on, you'd better bring her in here.'

The Doctor, realising he was the 'you' in question and the shop was the 'here' in question, took the woman's purple-hued arm and led her inside.

'Welcome to the club.' The miserable voice came from a bright yellow young man. He was yellow from hair to shoes, taking in everything in between. The Doctor assumed from his yellow apron that he belonged to the shop. Also present were a red man

with a red dog, two green schoolgirls in green school uniform, several indigo shoppers and a thoroughly violet policeman. They were huddled unhappily between racks of still-green cabbages and cucumbers and courgettes.

'Blimey!' said the Doctor. He whipped out his glasses and began to peer closely at the multicoloured individuals, eliciting peals of giggles from the schoolgirls.

The other people didn't laugh. 'Are you really a doctor?' the violet old lady asked nervously.

A few heads shot up at that. 'A doctor? Can you help us?'

'Oh, I expect so,' said the Doctor cheerfully. 'I can find solutions for most things. Now, I suppose you have all tried soap and water...? No, no, don't glare at me like that, I was just asking. Tell you what, why don't you tell me exactly what happened here...'

I t had only happened a short time before – ten minutes ago, one of the girls said, but Ted thought it was a bit longer than that; he could work it out because he'd been due a tea break. Ted, the greengrocer's assistant – now the yellow man – had been arranging pineapples on the displays outside the shop. People had shouted, and he'd turned to see something zooming from the sky towards him. He hadn't even had time to wonder what was happening – vague thoughts of a missile or a meteorite had only just begun to cross his mind when the rainbow hit.

'It took a few moments to realise that I was OK,' he said. 'I thought it was going to explode or something, but I couldn't move my legs to run... Then, I don't know why – I wasn't really thinking straight – I put out a hand to it. I think I just wanted to see if I could touch it. You see – well, you probably did see, out there – it looked solid, but not. And it went right through the fruit stand, but hadn't broken it. I don't know how to describe it. Sort of like... solid light.'

'Solid light,' echoed the Doctor. 'Yes, I see what you mean. So did it feel solid?'

Ted nodded. But 'not really,' put in the red man.

'A bit fizzy,' said one of the girls.

'More sort of fuzzy,' said the other.

The Doctor turned the conversation back to Ted, who held up his hands. 'I was wearing gloves,' the greengrocer's assistant said, 'cos of handling the fruit. And where I was touching the rainbow, my glove began to turn the same colour. Like it was infecting it, or something.'

'He yelled, and I came over to help, and look what happened!' said the red man.

'Rrufff!' added his dog.

'I took off my glove but my hand was going yellow too!' said Ted.

'And then it spread all over you...' said the Doctor. 'Now, let me guess – you'd been touching what we'll call the yellow "stripe" of the rainbow. And when you came along –' he turned to the red man – 'you touched the outer rim, which is red. Hands up everyone who turned the same colour as the "stripe" they touched.'

All hands rose in the air.

'Right, right,' muttered the Doctor. 'Hmm, I wonder what would happen if you touched two different colours at the same time...'

He turned as if to leave. 'No, no!' called his audience.

'Oh, all right. But aren't you fascinated? It's fascinating, you should be fascinated! Red turns you red, orange turns you orange – lumps your clothes in with you but it's not spreading any further than that, you're not turning your chairs yellow or anything. It affects dogs and cats and bananas, but it doesn't seem to be hurting anyone. Which is good.'

Without a sound, the old lady and the policeman fell to the floor.

The schoolgirls shrieked in alarm. The Doctor dived towards the two people on the ground, grabbing the old lady's wrist to take her pulse while simultaneously putting his head on the policeman's chest and listening intently. 'It's all right, two hearts beating,' he said after a moment. 'That's one each, I mean.' He stood up. 'They're fine. Just... unconscious.'

'You've gotta help 'em!' cried Ted. 'You're a doctor!'

The Doctor shrugged. 'Perhaps if I –'

He was cut off by a scream from outside the shop. Then came another and another. The Doctor dashed to the door and flung it open; the shop bell rang out violently. He stared out as his multicoloured companions crowded behind him, the two green girls standing on tiptoes to try to see over his shoulder.

Colour was seeping from the base of the rainbow. Expanding pools dyed everything in their path red, orange, yellow, green, blue, indigo or violet. The people who had been crowding around excitedly were now trying to flee, but those closest to the rainbow could not get away fast enough. They screamed and yelled as the hues hit, as shoes changed colour and the tints advanced up feet, ankles and legs.

The Doctor hurriedly moved back as the greengrocer dived for the shop door. The man was already blue up to his knees. With a curse, he slammed the door shut behind him, but a sea of colour was already oozing underneath: red with edges of orange.

'Everyone back!' called the Doctor, although they didn't need to be told – the greengrocer had opened a door at the rear of the shop and they were all heading through it into a storeroom. The Doctor himself paused to pick up the unconscious old lady and bring her through, then went back for the policeman.

The red pool had got there first – but it didn't seem to affect the man. He remained a brilliant, unmistakable violet while the red passed underneath him. Even so, the Doctor took hold of the policeman's hands and began to drag him away.

The Doctor turned his head, looking over his shoulder to set a course for the storeroom door. Suddenly his burden seemed extraordinarily light. His hands were no longer gripping the policeman's calloused palms. He clutched at thin air and turned to see that the man was... no longer there. No longer there at all.

There were yells of surprise coming from the storeroom, and when the Doctor hurried in he was unsurprised to discover that the old lady had vanished too. 'She just disappeared!' said Ted. 'One second she was there, next second she wasn't!' He took a deep breath. 'Well, at least the rest of us are all right.'

As he spoke, the indigo-coloured shoppers sank to the floor.

And a pool of red began to seep under the door.

The greengrocer yelped and jumped back, like a beachgoer scared of being washed away by the incoming tide.

'Don't worry,' said the Doctor. 'Once the rainbow's made its mark, it looks like that's it.' He nodded his head towards the greengrocer's assistant, who was nearest to the entrance. Without Ted noticing, the red had already reached him. But like the unconscious policeman before him, the colour had passed him by. He retained his original hue; no red tinted the bright sunny yellow that covered him from head to foot.

'There,' the Doctor continued. 'Once it's got you – it's got you. It's just –' He scrambled on to an empty crate – 'it hasn't got me yet. And I don't want to seem selfish, but if I'm going to sort this out, it might be better if it doesn't.'

'You've not done much sorting out so far!' said Ted. 'Look at me! I look like a banana!'

'I think that old woman melted,' one of the schoolgirls said dully, too traumatised to be anything other than matter-of-fact. 'I think this is like acid and it's melting us on the inside, and you fall over when it hits your brain and then you just totally melt away into nothing.' She stared into the distance, tears hovering in the corners of her eyes. Her friend began to sob.

For several minutes, the others crowded round to comfort the two girls, the Doctor occasionally putting in an unenthusiastic 'there, there' from his crate-top perch. Ted had been right, he wasn't doing a lot to help. He had to think of something, and soon. Keeping out of the way, on top of a box – that wasn't the Doctor's way of doing things.

'Anyway,' the red man said at last. 'I don't think it can be acid. If my brain was melting, I think I'd know about it.' He didn't sound too sure, though, glancing at the Doctor for confirmation.

'Yeah, no melting brains – that violet couple seemed perfectly normal when I examined them,' the Doctor replied distractedly,

climbing on to a chair as the red began to bleed up his wooden crate.

'But they did just fall over,' put in Ted. 'And then that lot, too.' He wrinkled his nose towards the unconscious indigo shoppers. 'I could be next!'

'You won't be next,' said the sad schoolgirl. 'Mr Cousins will.' She looked at the greengrocer.

'What?' the man yelled.

The Doctor was nodding his head eagerly. 'Oh, of course! It's so obvious! Well done,' he said to the girl. 'A clear sequence. Backwards rainbow! Everyone who's violet falls over, then vanishes. Indigo after that. Next comes blue –' he pointed a finger at Mr Cousins the greengrocer – 'green –' he smiled apologetically at the two girls as he pointed at them – 'yellow –' Ted's turn – 'orange and finally red.' His finger indicated the red man and his dog.

'I'm next!' Mr Cousins was still yelling. 'Oh blimey, I'm next – where's a phone, I've got to call Mary, oh help me, please help me...' His voice trailed off as he realised the Doctor wasn't listening.

'I need a watch, anyone got a watch?' the Doctor was saying, suddenly alive again. 'Anyone know what time they fell over? I reckon it's about ten minutes.' He pointed over towards where the indigo people lay – where they had lain. They were gone. 'Quick!' he cried, catching the watch that the red man threw to him. 'How long will it be, how long will it be?'

'How long will what be?' asked the red man.

'That,' said the Doctor. Mr Cousins had fallen heavily to the floor, his head smashing into a pile of over-ripe peaches. 'About ten seconds between one colour vanishing and the next falling over.'

'Does that matter?' cried Ted, wiping a splash of peach juice off his face. 'He was really scared – and all you did was time him! You don't have to worry, you've not even been affected...'

'Sorry,' said the Doctor, 'but I couldn't have saved him. I don't even know what's happening, not yet. But knowing that there's a

ten-second gap – that might come in handy, somewhere down the line. Course, it might not. I don't have any answers yet.' The red was halfway up the legs of his chair now, and he hopped on to a pile of sacks of potatoes instead. For a second he wobbled, then he righted himself.

And then he suddenly stood tall. 'I don't have answers yet, but I'm going to find them. Better red than dead, they say...'

He jumped on to the red floor. 'Red should be the last colour,' he said, as his trainers began to turn scarlet. 'So I reckon I've got just over half an hour to save the world.' He sprinted away.

'But where're you going?' Ted called after him.

A voice floated back: 'Somewhere over the rainbow...'

The substance of the rainbow was... odd, solid but insubstantial at the same time, and the Doctor could see why no-one had been able to describe it. He was able to grasp it, though, and pull himself up – although he was careful not to grip too hard, fearing that his hands might go right through and he'd find himself falling to the ground. And the ground was, by now, a fair distance below. He thought he spotted a tiny police box – now a vibrant green – and wished he was travelling by that instead. But this had seemed the only way.

He hadn't been achieving anything back in the greengrocer's shop. As far as he could see, there was nothing to discover at that end of the rainbow.

But of course rainbows have two ends. The only place he could think of looking for answers was the other end of the rainbow. If he was lucky, he might even find a crock of gold!

To find the other end, as quickly and simply as possible, he needed to go as the crow flies, without all the buildings and trees that obscured his view and his path. So he had to climb the rainbow.

The red had been creeping up over his feet when he started his climb, but it was now on his knees and hands too, where he was gripping the outside edge of the bow. It looked like he was wearing crimson gloves.

That wasn't worrying him, because he hadn't really had a choice. What was worrying him was time. He was quick and sure, but the climb wasn't that easy – although it had turned into an almost horizontal crawl now, which meant he was close to the top of the arch. The trouble was – he glanced swiftly at the red man's watch, now on his own red wrist – that he'd used up a lot of his time.

He sighed, and stood up. With a red hand, he shielded his eyes – still, thankfully, their natural light brown – and surveyed the landscape. The rainbow's end was far off; somewhere in the middle of a cluster of high-rise buildings, he thought.

He looked again at the watch, and sat down. There was only one thing for it...

And with a cry of 'wheeeeee!', like a child gliding down the world's longest banister, the Doctor slid down the rainbow....

He'd been right, the end was in the middle of that cluster of high-rise buildings. What he'd failed to take into account was that the end might be actually *inside* one of the buildings. As he approached – very fast – he could see that the rainbow sliced straight through a sloping roof. Anyone hitting that roof at high speed would, if they weren't killed by the impact, find themselves rolling down the slope and then falling off the edge, which was, ooh, about twenty storeys off the ground.

But he couldn't stop now!

Crossing two red fingers, and calling out 'Don't try this at home!' – just in case any children were watching – the Doctor plunged on downwards...

...and found himself carried through the roof, through a cobwebby and deserted attic, through a series of empty kitchens and bathrooms and bedrooms, until he finally came to earth with a thump on a threadbare beige carpet.

His first thought was how unusual and strange it was to feel excited about seeing the colour beige. His second was a realisation that someone was screaming at him.

He looked up at the young girl who had just witnessed a bright red stranger fall through the ceiling into her bedroom. 'Hello!' he said with a grin.

It took a few moments for the girl to stop screaming, during which time the Doctor picked himself up and examined the room. He found what he was looking for almost immediately. The end of

the rainbow. And at the end of the rainbow, a crock of gold. Well, almost.

Sitting on a small wooden desk was a gold-coloured rock with a crack in it, and shooting out of the crack was a series of lights: red, orange, yellow, green, blue, indigo, violet. The shafts of light weaved together and expanded into the rainbow on which the Doctor had arrived. There were no pools of colour here, though, and the only brightly hued thing about the girl herself was her rich auburn hair. However he did spot a few unnaturally gaudy items here and there: a red teddy bear, some orange magazines and pens, a red clock, a small portable television that was also red. Nothing between yellow and violet in the spectrum. That didn't give him much time.

Now the girl was no longer screaming, the Doctor turned to her again. 'I'm the Doctor,' he said.

The girl was calmer now. 'I'm Bobby.' She pointed at the rock. 'Is that yours? I'm really sorry –'

The Doctor shook his head. 'Not mine.'

She raised her eyebrows. 'Oh! I thought...' She gestured uncomfortably at his red hair, his red face, his red clothes.

'The tomato look? I'll tell you about that in a minute. But first you're gonna have to tell me everything. Because I'm here to sort it all out, but I'm in a hurry. A big hurry.'

So Bobby told him everything.

'I found it in the park. That rock thing. There was a gleam, like gold, and there it was in a flower bed. I don't think it had been there very long, because it had broken some flower stems and the flowers weren't quite dead yet. And I think it must have been dropped, maybe from quite high up, because it had broken so many flowers and sunk into the earth a bit too.'

'Nice bit of noticing,' the Doctor said, nodding approvingly.

'I looked around but I couldn't see anyone who might have dropped it, and there weren't any footprints in the flower bed except mine. So I picked it up, because I wanted to see what it was. And when my thumb pressed into it, a blue beam shot out, like a laser, and turned a daffodil blue. I did it again, and it happened again. And if I pressed it in different places, different coloured beams came out. All the colours of the rainbow...

'And I thought... I thought... well, I thought if it didn't belong to anyone I could bring it home and maybe use it. You know, on my hair.'

The Doctor looked at her blankly.

'My Mum won't let me dye it,' she said. 'But I bet this'd work.'

The Doctor was making a 'what?' face.

'To change the colour!' she said. 'So it's not red any more!'

'As a disguise?' the Doctor suggested.

'No! So I don't get called names. Or – well, worse stuff.'

'Blimey! They must be jealous, that's what it is.' The Doctor looked wistful. 'I've always wanted to be ginger... Anyway, so you brought this rock home?'

'Mm. I saw it had a crack in it – just a thin one, like a thread. Probably cos it'd been dropped, I thought. And I had it in my bedroom, and I was testing it, you know, on stuff, before I did my hair. And then I saw the crack, and it seemed a bit bigger but I thought I was just remembering it wrong, so I carried on. And then – and then...'

'It cracked right open and a rainbow shot out of it?' guessed the Doctor.

Bobby nodded. 'Right through the ceiling. At least I knew there wouldn't be anyone up there, the people above us don't get home till late. But then things started disappearing, and I didn't know what to do...'

While she'd been telling her story, the Doctor had been examining the gold rock. 'I don't know what to do either,' he said, and told her, as quickly as he could, what was happening at the other end of the rainbow. 'But,' he added, 'at least I know now why it's happening.'

'You do?'

'Got a good guess, anyway.' He leaned towards the rock and pointed the sonic screwdriver at it. 'This – the rock, not my sonic screwdriver – belongs to some people called the Filbiks. They like collecting things and classifying things and looking at things. They have museums and exhibitions like you have telly. So a Filbik expedition'll visit a planet to collect stuff, use one of those to mark their specimens – red for fish, orange for beetles, yellow for rocks, that sort of thing. When the mark's activated, it gives off a low-level dose of a sedative, to stop the living things from getting distressed, and then everything's beamed up to their ship, category by category. This marker's been dropped from a passing ship, I reckon, and the damage has allowed the marking beams to escape.'

With a final *bzzzz* from the sonic screwdriver, the crack in the rock sealed itself and the rainbow vanished. 'There. At least no-one else'll be affected. That's better than a kick in the teeth. Right, where was I? Yeah, everything's getting marked, and given a huge dose of the sedative, and then collected...' He suddenly stopped, alarmed. 'Magazines! They can't get sedated! Or pens!'

'Well, no,' she said, and for the first time in all this strangeness she was looking at him as if he'd said something really stupid.

'I mean, that was how I'd been counting things, before. Unconscious, vanish; next colour, unconscious, vanish. But the only orange things here are magazines and pens! They could have been

unconscious for ages and I'd never know! Quick – did you colour anything yellow?'

'Yes.'

'And when did they disappear – the yellow things?'

'Oh, just before you arrived.'

He looked in horror at the red man's red watch. 'And I've been running on for ages! Any second now...'

And as if he'd reminded them that it was about time they were off, the orange magazines and pens vanished.

The Doctor began to speak as fast as he could, his eyes never leaving the watch. 'I'm going to fall unconscious in ten seconds' time. I'll try to fight it, but I probably won't succeed. I'll be transported to the ship. No-one else knows what it's all about, just you. You have to find a way of contacting the Filbiks, or we'll all end up in a museum forever. It's all up to you...'

...and he dropped to the floor.

H e'd fallen unconscious suddenly, instantaneously, with no awareness of it. Coming round was more like waking from a heavy sleep. The Doctor, normally so alert, couldn't quite work out where he was. The TARDIS? No, but there were banks of switches and computer screens, so it might be some sort of spaceship. And there was a girl there – had he been travelling with anyone? There had been a red-haired woman, not that long ago – but their hair hadn't been that red. That bright, pillar-box, traffic-light, primary red.

Then he was conscious again, and he remembered. He sprang to his feet. 'Bobby! Quick! Lots to do! People to save!'

'It's all right,' she said shyly. 'I've talked to the Filbiks. It's all gonna be OK.'

The Doctor boggled. 'You've talked to the Filbiks?'

'Yes.'

'And it's all going to be OK?'

'Uh-huh.'

'I think,' said the Doctor, 'that it might be an idea if, once again, you told me everything.'

She began to explain. 'You said I had to talk to them, these aliens, but I didn't know how. I thought if I could get to their ship... But the only way of getting to the ship was to have one of those marks and be collected with the other red things. So...' She indicated the gold rock, lying on a computer bank, then pointed with a grin at her hair. 'I used the rock and marked myself. I thought I wouldn't get such a big dose of sleepy stuff if it was only a little mark, not red all over like you were.'

The Doctor looked down at himself, and realised that he was once again dressed in a brown suit. His hands were their normal pinky colour, and the watch on his wrist was gold.

'This is just a storage ship, they fill it up and then drag it home, like a trailer. But there are controls here, and a telephone sort of thing to the main ship. I talked to them on that. They told me how to remove the colour, and I was going to try to send everyone home when you woke up.' She pointed at a magazine and a pen. 'Got those from the orange section, so I could write down their instructions. But –' she gave him a lop-sided grin – 'maybe you could do it instead. I reckon you'd find it easier to understand their instructions. It all got a bit technical, and I don't want to get it wrong.'

The Doctor was grinning. 'Wrong? I don't think you could get things wrong if you tried! This is brilliant. You're brilliant. Your hair's brilliant!'

She laughed. 'Yeah. I think I'm going to keep it. Bit of a statement. I'm choosing to be red. Not gonna hide it. They don't like it, it's their problem.'

'Good one,' said the Doctor.

'Mind you,' Bobby added, 'my mum'll go crazy...'

The Doctor inspected the ship's storage chambers before attempting to send anything back to Earth. He found all his companions from the greengrocer's shop, although it took a few moments to recognise them without their distinctive colourisation. They were still unconscious. 'Not got a Time Lord's constitution,' he commented. 'Just as well – we won't have to explain anything, and hopefully they'll be too groggy when they come round to remember much of this.'

The things from Earth were all in different sections, thanks to the malfunctioning marker-rock. The Doctor found previously yellow Ted on a shelf surrounded by birds; Bobby oohed with delight over the strange, alien species there. The policeman and the old lady, who'd been coloured violet, were in a storeroom full of reptiles. Huddled by a collection of flowers were the red man and his dog; the Doctor strapped the man's watch back to his wrist. Bobby seized a teddy bear from nearby. 'It's mine,' she said. 'I'd turned it red. This is the room we both arrived in, actually. I dragged you through to the control room with me – it was quite tricky – you see, I hoped you'd wake up so I wouldn't have to do anything. But when you didn't – I did.'

The formerly red man shifted slightly, giving out a slight grumble in his sleep. 'And talking of doing things, we'd better be,' said the Doctor hurriedly. 'Doing things, I mean. Because I really really hate having to explain things to people, they keep on and on and on...'

He was already halfway back to the control room. Bobby hurried after him. When he got there, he picked up the magazine and skimmed the notes that were written in between the lines of an article about How To Tell If A Boy Fancies You.

'Right. Plug in device...' He inserted the gold rock into an opening that seemed designed to hold it. 'Turn on auxiliary power... reverse magnetic function to maximum... see if he makes excuses to sit next to you in class – no, that's not it, ah, here – bron-kel level 4.7836...' He carried on, flicking switches and inputting values into a keyboard. Finally a diagram popped up on a screen, each specimen noted and numbered. 'Right, here we go,' he said.

'How will you know which are the right ones to send back?' Bobby asked. 'Do we have to go and check all their numbers?'

'Nope,' said the Doctor, 'don't tell the Filbiks, but I think I might just accidentally send everything back while I'm here. And maybe sabotage the collecting equipment too, well, some of it. Rocks and flowers I can cope with, but birds and fish? Where d'you think they'd rather be, back home doing the flying and swimming thing, or stuck in an exhibition somewhere?'

Bobby grinned, but looked a bit nervous too. 'Won't the Filbiks be cross? They were nice, too, they did help me sort things out, you know.'

'Yeah. But they'll get over it. Maybe we can leave 'em your telly, get them hooked on *The X Factor* instead, give 'em a new interest in life.' The Doctor pointed towards the door. 'Better go and find your spot, Bobby. Can't reverse your trip if you're not in the place where you arrived.'

Now she frowned. 'But what about you? How will you get back if you have to operate the controls?'

'No problemo. Just need to make sure I don't return absolutely everything in the green section,' he said. 'Go on. Off you go.'

She looked reluctant, but headed off anyway. As she reached the door, he called after her. 'You were a star. A real star.' He picked up the magazine and threw it for her to catch. 'You might be needing this. All the boys'll be fancying you with that hair.'

'Yeah,' she said. 'Yeah, maybe they will. They'll have to watch out for my "fiery temper", though. It's gotta be a lot worse with hair this bright.' She smiled. 'Bye, Doctor.'

'Bye, Bobby.' The Doctor turned back to his task. The shiny screen acted like a mirror, and he caught a glimpse of his own hair, now back to its regular brown.

Oh well, he thought. Maybe next time he'd be ginger.

But he hoped he had a while to go before he found out...

Scared Stiff

WRITTEN BY **MARK GATISS**   ILLUSTRATIONS BY **BEN WILLSHER**

Dennis Bridger had a headache. This was not, in itself, unusual. He always enjoyed a tipple or two after a show but the old house where they'd recorded the latest programme had offered nothing more than milky tea and some Jaffa Cakes that should have been eaten by the previous January. So it wouldn't have surprised anyone if he'd asked his assistant Tonya to nip down to the offie for a bottle of Scotch. After all, being possessed by a limping Victorian child, a fire-and-brimstone Puritan and a strange old man with a tam o'shanter can take it out of a man. But he'd not had any booze this time. Not a drop.

Throwing back the duvet, Dennis sat up, only half noticing that he'd gone to bed in his underpants and a solitary sock. His tongue was like a stick, there was a throbbing tightness behind his eyes and, when he moved it, his neck made a noise like someone stepping on a bag of crisps. Had the dream come again? The voices? Dennis winced. Maybe he'd overdone the possession.

He gave a phlegmy cough – dice rattling in a cup – dragged on his discarded trousers and flicked on the kettle, the bleak dawn a grey strip through the cheap hotel curtains. Where was he? Cheltenham? Somewhere like that? He'd lost track. Hotels all looked the same.

The tea he brewed was weak and colourless as pencil-shavings. But the biscuits were nice. They had little bits of ginger in them. Dennis glanced at the watch on his freckled wrist. Too late for breakfast. He was always too late for breakfast.

Cheltenham! What did Cheltenham hold for him? Was it that sixteenth-century coaching inn haunted by an evil Squire? Or the old schoolroom where people swore they could hear kiddies' footsteps? Of course, Dennis wasn't supposed to know any of these details but Tonya secretly Googled up all the spooks for which the various places were famous. Then, on the show itself, Dennis could confidently and melodramatically get himself possessed by a couple of them. Hence the stiff neck. The fire-and-brimstone Puritan with all his *thees* and *thous* and shouting his head off about the wrath of the Lord had gone down well. Corynne had actually looked a bit scared. He liked it when Corynne got scared.

But lately he'd felt odd. Different. He had dreams of a yawning chasm. A chasm that was closing. And voices that seemed to want something from him. Could it be, after all those years living hand to mouth and trailing round half empty theatres, Dennis Bridger was discovering he had real psychic powers? Then it hit him, making his pounding head pound even more. Cheltenham! Oh God. The

Shuffling into the bathroom, Dennis made a quick examination of his pouchy face in the mottled mirror and had a shower – the spray as weak as baby's dribble. He needed to make an effort. Look his best for the live show. Corynne would murder him otherwise. And Corynne was not to be crossed.

'And that's what you heard? A sort of whispering?'

'Yeah. Or singing. Sometimes it's like… singing.'

'And what have people seen?'

'Well, there's been loads more sightings lately. Things moving in the shadows. And…well, skeletons.'

Corynne Fletcher nodded enthusiastically. 'Great. Say it like that tonight and you'll give everyone goose-bumps!'

She patted the fat girl on the arm and then swept off down the stone corridor, her long black coat trailing behind her. She pulled up short and gave a little yell as a pale man in a red jumper loomed up in front of her.

'God, Simon, you made me jump!'

'Sorry,' whispered Simon. His voice sounded like steam escaping. 'I've got news about Dennis.' He dragged out the 's' of Dennis.

'Oh?' Corynne's eyes were thick with eye-liner. They narrowed dangerously.

'Bit worse for wear last night,' shushed Simon.

'*Great.*'

'Tonya says he wasn't himself at all. Like he was… possessed.'

'Ha, *ha.*' Corrine huffed. 'Where is he now?'

'At the Travelodge. Communing with the spirits, he says.'

'Whiskey or brandy?'

Simon laughed weakly, then put a bony finger to his lips. 'Sorry. I shouldn't laugh should I? It's important this show, innit?'

Corynne smoothed down her black top and tutted at the dandruff she found there. 'Yes, Simon. Very important. If you and I still want to be employed by this time next week.'

Simon looked worried, making his already long face look even glummer. Corynne put a hand on his arm. 'Not to worry. Dennis'll come through for us. He always does. Now where's Pat?'

'Having a fit out the back. She says her Clarins has dried out.'

Corynne strode off again. When the cameras shifted to night-vision, the horrible green light made Corynne look like a ghost herself. 'For God's sake!' she'd said to Pat after viewing the last programme. 'Get more slap on me!'

But Pat wasn't confident. No-one was anymore. Corynne's show *Scared Stiff* had been running successfully for over five years without a hitch. But now the hitch had come. And his name was Preston Gilchrist.

◆◇◆

'Is this your card?'

Tonya's eyes grew saucer-wide. 'Yeah!' she squeaked, delighted. 'That's amaaaazing!'

'All part of the service,' smiled the tubby man in the shiny waistcoat. 'And how may I enthral you next, goodly wench?'

Tonya had noticed that before. Preston Gilchrist peppered his speech with funny little old-fashioned sayings, like he was Shakespeare or something. He'd been calling Simon 'sirrah' all morning, and when they'd met in the pub the night before, he'd asked the confused barman for 'four pints of your finest frothing ale'. Tonya found it a bit annoying but Preston was okay, really. He was brilliant at magic tricks (like the one he'd just shown her) and he knew everything there was to know about Spiritualism and mediums and all that stuff. But that was the problem. He knew too much.

Crooked House
by
Mark Gatiss

Preston stroked his wispy beard with one hand and flashily cut the cards with the other. He was small and overweight and his greasy hair hung down his back. With his paisley bow-tie and waistcoat, Tonya reckoned he fancied himself as resembling a vampire killer or something, like in the Hammer films, but really he just looked like an idiot.

'What're you going to say… tonight?' asked Tonya, haltingly.

'*Pardonnez moi*, madame?'

'On the show. You're not going to try and show Dennis up again are you?'

Preston laid a hand on his heart. '*Would* I?'

'Yes!' cried Tonya, scratching her knee. There was a hole in her tights and her flesh showed through like a white coin. 'It was awful last time. I don't think he's got over it.'

Preston gave a smug smile. 'Well, that's what comes of being a fraud.'

Tonya felt her face colour. 'He's not a fraud!'

'My dear,' said Preston insufferably. 'When you've seen as many fake mediums as my good self, it's not hard to spot. Dennis Bridger has got it coming.'

'He's not a fraud,' repeated Tonya, glumly. 'I mean, we help him out a bit, cos it's telly and there's no time to prepare, but Dennis is the real thing. He's the seventh son of a seventh son.'

'I thought that was werewolves.'

'You know what I mean! He's got the gift. He really has. I've seen him do amazing things.'

Preston shrugged. Then, all at once, his watery eyes grew smaller as he peered over Tonya's shoulder. 'Wait. Wait a minute. There's… there's someone there!'

'Don't!' said Tonya sharply.

'No. I'm not kidding. Old man. White hair. God, I can… I can hear his voice…'

Tonya looked round. 'Stop it, Preston.'

Preston gave a low groan and his head slumped onto his chest. Then it snapped up again. 'William? Henry? Or George? Is it George?'

Tonya cocked her head.

'Did you… did you know a George?' asked Preston.

'Yeah,' said Tonya, carefully. 'My Dad's uncle. We used to go round his house when we were little.'

Preston nodded sagely. 'Uncle George. He's smiling, Tonya. He says he used to love sitting in his chair and listening to you laugh. And those long white socks you wore. Always falling down…'

Tonya felt herself smiling. She'd loved her Uncle George.

Preston nodded again. 'He wants you to know he's very happy, Tonya. And you're not to worry about your finances.'

Tonya gasped. How did he know about *that*? It must be true. Her late Uncle George was talking through Preston!

'He's going now, Tonya,' murmured Preston dreamily. 'Going. But he says he'll always remember that day you cried when you won the school sprint…'

Tonya made a little sobbing sound.

'…and that he's just as proud of you now as he was then.' Preston's voice trailed off and his head slumped onto his chest again.

Tonya came and sat by him. 'My God! You've got the Gift as well! It must be this place. The old Abbey!'

Preston suddenly straightened, picked up the deck of cards and spread them in a fan as wide as his smile. 'Smoke and mirrors, my goodly wench. Just Victorian parlour tricks. They never fail.'

'Eh?'

'Who doesn't know a white-haired old man called George? Grandad. Grandad's friend. Someone. Probably dead. If you'd said William or Alfred or Henry, I'd have gone for that. People only latch onto the bits they want to hear.'

Tonya felt like she'd been slapped. 'But what about the running race? And I'm dead worried about my bank balance!'

'Of course you are,' said Preston smoothly. 'The show might be cancelled, mightn't it? And last night in the bar? You told me you'd run for your county when you were a teenager.'

'Did I?' Tonya couldn't remember much after the fourth Merlot.

Preston shrugged again and his cheap waistcoat rode up over his tummy.

Tonya let her fingers idly stroke the hole in her tights. 'I feel such a fool. You won't... you won't do anything like that tonight, will you?'

'Who can say?' Preston Gilchrist chuckled unpleasantly. 'Depends what materialises.'

A tiny, round webcam was focussed on one wall of the Abbey crypt. It wasn't showing anything to the viewers at home just yet. In truth there was nothing to see. Just a damp old wall with big patches of moss.

But then something did stir in the tar-black shadows. A crooked figure inched forward, mouldered clothing clinging to its ancient bones. Wreathed in a strange, bluish light, the skeleton shambled towards the stairway, the bones of its feet clacking on each weathered step.

A few moments after it disappeared from sight, a tall blue box appeared out of thin air.

Corynne wiped sweat from her upper lip. 'More, Pat. Don't be afraid.'

Pat made a face and dabbed at Corynne's cheek with a powder puff. 'It's ladled on like custard as it is, love. You'll frighten the punters.'

Corynne glanced over Pat's chunky shoulder at the three hundred-strong audience that were filing into the Abbey. It was cold and they were all in anoraks or thick winter coats, their breath drifting about them like ectoplasm. The low temperature helped, of course. It looked great on screen and, by the time Dennis and Corynne held the séance in the old Abbey crypt, the eager crowd would be so keyed up they'd believe anything. She hoped.

'Two minutes,' said a tinny voice in Corynne's ear.

She nodded and made a thumbs-up sign to the nearest camera. Everything was going to be fine. The Abbey was a great location. It was Hallowe'en. People had been seeing ghosts there since records began. And now these sightings of skeletons! It was too good to be true. Most important of all, she'd visited Dennis in his dressing room and he was confident he could stand up to that little twit Gilchrist. Corynne knew what was behind it, of course. Board-room power struggles at Breezy-TV, the show's network. Big boss Clive hated Scared Stiff and wanted it off the air. So he'd replaced their regular, soft-hearted sceptic with this arrogant little magician who was obviously set on getting a show of his own. She'd seen trouble coming, all through the last live show from that draughty Scottish castle – what was it called? – but nothing could have prepared her for Preston Gilchrist's viciousness. He'd demolished poor Dennis. Every croaky voice he'd done, every tic of his face, every supposed 'fact' about the spirits that haunted the place had been ripped apart with grisly precision, leaving the nation's favourite medium totally exposed. Corynne had never really got on with Dennis. She didn't like his wandering hands or his Benson and Hedges breath or his roguish Mancunian 'charm'. But she knew a good thing when she saw one and Dennis's clever tricks had helped them become Breezy-TV's number one show. She couldn't bear to think it might all be over. The show was her life. Besides, she'd just put down the deposit on a five bedroom show home in Barnes...

Preston Gilchrist was on a roll.
He knew it. Humiliating Dennis
Bridger was just the beginning.
Soon Breezy-TV would give him
his own programme. His old mate Clive had promised. A
whole new style of show. A bit of magic, bit of psychic debunking,
bit of glamour. Like David Nixon used to do when Preston was a
kid. And girls. Lots of girls. He'd see that Tonya all right, as well.
She was lovely. Deserved better than to be stuck with an old fraud
like Bridger.

Yes, he was on a hell of a roll. As Preston swaggered down the
dingy stone corridor towards the cameras he was even composing
the theme tune to his new show. He whistled a few bars and then
gave one last, high pitched squeal as a skeletal hand shot out of the
shadows and broke his neck.

◆◄◆►◆

The tinny voice began to count down in Corynne's ear and she
turned, smiling, to the camera.

'Ratchett Abbey,' she intoned. 'The most haunted place in Britain?
Scared Stiff is live here, this Hallowe'en night. Join me, Corynne
Fletcher, and psychic medium Dennis Bridger, as we delve into the
mysteries of this truly terrifying location!'

The theme music belted out as the audience applauded; speeded up
shots of various desolate ruins and the night-cam visions of Corynne
that made her look ghastly streaming across the monitors. Corynne
caught a glimpse of her reflection and shuddered. God, she looked
rough. Maybe it wouldn't be so bad if the show was pulled. At least
she'd get a holiday.

Her face had fallen and she realised with a start that she was back
on-air, only plastering on a smile in the nick of time.

'Hello! And welcome again to *Scared Stiff*. We've got remote
cameras all over the Abbey, Pete's standing by as usual to take all

be hiding in the shadows! And actually, we've
got a caller on already. Hello? Is that Mandy?'

A telephone line crackled and a thin voice
said: '*Hello?*'

'Hi. It's Mandy, isn't it?'

'*Hi, Corynne! I'm a big fan of the show. We've been watching
since the beginning.*'

A dog yapped in the background.

'*Hush, Monty!*'

'Yes,' cut in Corynne. 'And you've seen something haven't you,
Mandy?'

'*Yes!*' said Mandy enthusiastically. '*On the webcam in Room
Three. Like white smoke. Drifting about. And it had a face in it,
I swear!*'

'A face!' said Corynne, giving a theatrical shudder.

The audience let out a big *wooooo!* and Corynne smiled warmly.
'Well, we'll get back to you on that one, Mandy, as soon as we've
looked at the tapes.'

'*There's something else,*' chipped in Mandy. '*Like a big box–*'

But Corynne cut her off. 'First, though, we're joined by our
resident sceptic. He certainly gave Dennis a run for his money last
time. Let's see what he's got in store this Hallowe'en night! Please
welcome – Preston Gilchrist!'

The chilly audience burst into applause and Corynne extended her
hand towards the arched entranceway. No-one came through it.

'Where are you, Preston?' called Corynne, turning her mouth
down like a sad clown.

The applause began to die and Corynne frowned. The tinny voice
in her ear hissed. '*Where is he? Where the hell's Preston?*'

And suddenly someone did come through the door. But it wasn't
the familiar tubby sceptic. It was a tall, skinny man in a tight-
fitting suit and trainers. He had big brown eyes and a rather hunted
expression. He wandered towards Corynne. 'You've got to stop this,'
was all he said.

'You're not Preston,' said Corynne.

'No.' The skinny man suddenly seemed to notice the cameras. 'No. I'm the Doctor.' He looked straight down the camera lens, grinned and sprawled in the chair next to Corynne. 'Doctor John Smith.'

No-one had come near Preston's body since the Doctor had emerged from the TARDIS and stumbled across it. He lay where he'd slumped, his head lolling horribly on his pigeon chest – just as it had when he'd pretended to be possessed for Tonya. Then, from out of the sepulchral gloom staggered the skeleton. Its work was done. Time for another, fresher body to take over. There was a whispering, chattering sound and a weird, writhing, spectral smoke began to pour from the skeleton's gaping jaw. It hung in the air for a moment, then streamed into Preston's dead mouth like inhaled cigarette smoke.

Preston's dead eyes flicked open.

The chubby corpse staggered to its feet and began to shuffle down the corridor. After a time, it came to the stone stairwell leading to the crypt. Preston needed help. Preston needed friends...

'Your friend – what was his name?'

'Preston,' said Coynne.

'Chubby fella. Waistcoat?'

'That's Preston.'

The Doctor smiled thinly. 'Preston's been... detained. So I'm filling in.'

Corynne gave a shrill laugh. The tinny voice in her ear-piece said: 'Go with it.'

'Is this... are we *live*?' asked the Doctor.

'Of course you are!' cried Corynne, over-brightly. 'Didn't Preston say? This is *Scared Stiff*!'

'I see,' said the Doctor – although he didn't. 'Soooo!' – he turned to Corynne. 'This place. Tell me all about it.'

Corynne shrugged. 'Ratchett Abbey. Built in the eleventh century. Dissolved by Henry VIII. Most haunted place in Britain.'

'Is it?' drawled the Doctor. 'Yes. I wouldn't be surprised. Not a bit surprised. Strange noises, half-glimpsed figures, cold patches, that sort of stuff?'

'Oh yes,' said Corynne. 'Our night-vision camera even picked up some orbs before we came on air'.

'Orbs?' said the Doctor, his face creasing into a frown that made his nose look sharper.

'Spectral organisms,' said Corynne, respectfully. 'Can we see that bit of footage?' She swung round in her chair and then bent towards the Doctor, covering her microphone. 'What the hell's going on?' she hissed in a low whisper.

'This is a weak point in space and time,' said the Doctor urgently.

'*What?*' snapped Corynne.

'I picked up the traces so I stopped off. There's something coming through here. You've got trouble.'

Simon gave a thumbs up sign to Corynne. The video clip was ready. 'Right!' she cried. 'Let's take a look at those strange orbs!'

The Doctor turned to the monitor. The picture was all green and white, shot with a night-vision camera. Dennis Bridger was wandering through a low, arched room and all around him floated strange little particles.

'So, Dr Sceptic!' cried Corynne. 'What do you make of that?'

The Doctor dismissed the pictures with an airy wave. 'Dust! That's just dust!'

'Really?' responded Corynne. 'Many psychic experts think– '

'It's *dust!* Look. Put your night-vision camera on and I'll go down there with a blackboard rubber and wave it about if you like! It's not dust I'm interested in. You need to take this programme off air.'

Corynne felt a surge of anger. *Clive*. One of Clive's tricks again. Well, they weren't going that easily. Not without a fight.

She turned to the camera. 'Well, we'll see about that. Join us for more spooky goings on at Ratchett Manor after the break!'

The brassy theme blared across the room. Corynne pulled out her ear-piece and stabbed her finger at the Doctor's chest. 'Look, mate. You can drop the act. If that jerk Clive wants the show off, why doesn't he have the guts to tell me to my face?'

The Doctor looked confused. 'What? Who's Clive?'

Simon in the red jumper bobbed into view. 'You okay, Corynne?'

'Fine. I'm fine.' She glared at the Doctor. 'So, come on. Talk.'

'There's a dead body out there in the corridor,' said the Doctor. 'I found it on the way in. Little bloke. Beard and long hair. Bow tie.'

'Preston!' cried Simon, shrilly.

The Doctor looked grim. 'Someone broke his neck.'

Corynne felt suddenly cold. 'But why? Why would anyone want to do that?'

'I'm not certain,' said the Doctor. 'But I think something needed him dead.'

'What do you mean some*thing*?'

The Doctor didn't answer.

Simon touched his fingers to his ear-piece and nodded. 'They've got that web-cam footage, Corynne. If you're interested?'

Corynne nodded vehemently. 'Show it, show it.'

Simon waved towards the monitor and a tape screed across it at high speed. It showed another poky stone room like all the others in the Abbey.

'Thanks for nothing, Mandy,' groaned Corynne. 'Is that it?'

'Wait,' said the Doctor. '*There!* Look! There!'

Corynne looked. There *was* something. Swirling about in the darkness like a comet. It disappeared for a moment then flared brightly and shot towards the camera. And for a moment – yes! – there was a face!

'Oh my God!' breathed Corynne.

The Doctor was on his feet. 'Have you got sound?'

Simon just stood there, dumbfounded.

'Quickly!' yelled the Doctor. 'Is there sound?'

The monitor suddenly gave a bang as the sound was activated. This was followed by a long, static hiss. There was something else in there. A voice. Choral. Almost like singing. But pleading, desperate…

'Louder!' shouted the Doctor.

'*Two minutes to end of ad break,*' said the voice in Corynne's ear.

Suddenly the monitor's volume leapt up. Corynne winced. But now they heard the voice at last.

'Pity us!' it groaned. 'Pity the Gelth!'

◆◇◆

The crypt was musty with the stink of ages. Through Preston's dead nostrils, the gaseous thing that inhabited his corpse luxuriated in the smell. It was glorious to feel again. To feel *something*. And time was growing short. This rift in Time and Space was tiny, as insubstantial as a shadow in a mirror. The others must come through. Find bodies. And together they would trace the host they had detected out there in the darkness. Sniffing out his psychic powers as Preston now inhaled the stench of the long dead.

With alien strength, he dragged open tombs not disturbed for hundreds of years, revealing skeletal remains within. And then he called to his brothers and sisters…

◆◇◆

'What the hell are they?' gasped Corynne.

'Met them before,' said the Doctor, his eyes darting from side to side. 'The Gelth. Remains of an alien species. They became gaseous to escape the destruction of their world. And they can only exist on this planet by inhabiting dead bodies.'

Corynne almost laughed. 'What, the living dead! Are you kidding?'

'No,' said the Doctor quietly. 'I'm not kidding.'

Simon put a nervous hand to his throat and tugged at his red jumper. 'Should… should we check on Preston?'

'Bit late,' said the Doctor, pacing about. 'He'll be walking.'

Corynne rubbed her weary face. Make-up came off all over her hands. 'Ok. I'll believe you. For now. So fill me in. You came here because you... detected something, right?'

'Right,' said the Doctor. 'A rift. Tiny version of a type I've seen before. The Gelth are on the other side of it. In another dimension. But the rift's closing. They haven't much time. They need to keep it open.'

Simon shook his head. 'This is mental. So... how do they keep this rift thing open?'

His voice was drowned out as a chilling scream cut through the even chillier air. Some of the audience were on their feet, hands pressed to their mouths. Dennis Bridger was standing in the arched entrance to the room. Behind him stood the ghastly pale corpse of Preston Gilchrist. Behind *him*... six mouldering skeletons, scraps of ancient clothing clinging to their blackened bones. And within their ribcages, swirling like fish in a tank, ghostly blue shapes, squealing, crying, weeping: 'Pity the Gelth! Pity the Gelth!'

'We're about to go back on air,' hissed Corynne urgently.

'Pull it!' yelled the Doctor.

'I can't!'

'You want millions of people to see ghostly extra-terrestrials invading the planet live on television?'

Corynne blinked. Then a slow smile spread across her pale face. '*Yes!* Of course I do!'

The Doctor shook his head. '*Humans.*'

Dennis Bridger still had a headache. But he didn't care. It was all true! He did have the Gift! The spirits had sought him out and they believed in him. And now it was his turn to help them.

He felt power surging through his body. It had all been worth it. All the cheap hotel rooms and psychic shows in tents that

smelled of grass and beer. All the jibes and the divorce and even the humiliation by Preston Gilchrist. What did it matter now? The whole world would see that he was the real thing.

And now he stood facing Corynne and, oh yes, she looked really scared this time! There was a stranger there too. A man in a brown suit, staring at him. Probably someone from Breezy-TV. You could almost hear his mind racing. Then, suddenly, the man broke into a broad smile. And started to laugh.

'Sorry! *Sorry*. I'm afraid you've been... Freaked Out!'

'What?' said Corynne.

But Dennis Bridger ignored the man, his face shining with joy. All those years. Pretending. Telling grieving people what they wanted to hear. Dennis Bridger. Putting on stupid voices. But now he had the chance to do something good. Help these poor lost souls come home!

The skeletal forms staggered slightly and the ghostly creatures within them writhed and belched and fizzed in anguish.

'Quickly!' hissed the dead mouth of Preston Gilchrist. 'No time! The rift is closing!'

Dennis saw Corynne push Simon towards the cameras. 'Are they getting this? Are they getting this?'

'Dennis Bridger!' laughed the man in the brown suit. 'Your face!'

Suddenly Dennis felt unsure again. What was this idiot going on about?

'Oooh!' mocked the man. 'Look at the funny skeletons! Happy Hallowe'en! You've been well and truly Freaked Out!'

Dennis frowned.

'What are you going on about?' hissed Corynne.

The Doctor's smile stayed in place but he whispered between clenched teeth: 'He's their medium. Keeping the rift open. Got to distract him. Go with it!'

Corynne nodded and stuck on a smile too. 'Yeah! Sorry, mate! *Freaked Out* is the new…um…'

'BBC show!' put in the Doctor.

'No! ITV3!' hissed Corynne under her breath. 'Tackier!' She raised her voice. 'Yeah! The new ITV3 show that turns the tables on celebs!'

'Yeah!' said the Doctor enthusiastically.

'No, no!' piped Simon. 'It's true! It's happening!'

'Bit of Hallowe'en fun!' cried the Doctor, stepping in front of him. 'Sorry, Stephen–'

'Simon.'

'*Simon!* Sorry! But you've been Freaked Out too!'

'But the skeletons…?'

'Just dummies!' said the Doctor, poking one of the monstrous creatures at his side. The Gelth within it snarled.

The Doctor tried not to look as worried as he felt. The rift *had* to close soon. Or the Gelth would do a good deal more than snarl…

◄◆►

'*Freaked Out?*' said Dennis quietly.

The Doctor nodded. 'Everyone's been in on it for months!'

Dennis Bridger looked down at himself. At the too-high trousers that covered his beer belly. At the packet of ciggies nestling in his shirt pocket. Who was he trying to kid? He glanced at the dreadful face of the supposedly dead Preston Gilchrist. Obviously just make-up, he thought.

'No! Noooo!' screamed Preston. 'Concentrate! Keep the rift open!'

But Dennis's mind was already wandering. He looked at the frightful skeletal things that surrounded him. Pretty convincing, he had to admit. But they could do anything with effects these days.

Closing his eyes, Dennis let the connection drift and the yawning hole he'd seen in his dreams began to close. He'd thought he'd felt the spirits pressing at it, urging it to open wider, wider. But that was just his imagination. Just another hangover that made his head hurt.

Then the special effects got really good. The skeletons around him shuddered and collapsed to the stone floor of the Abbey, shattering into dust. The ghosty things within them were sucked out and disappeared into the ether as though swirling down a drain. Preston Gilchrist stumbled and collapsed and it really looked as if a ghost leapt out of his mouth and then disappeared like the others.

Dennis rocked on his heels and felt the cold slap of reality. What a shame.

The audience were on their feet, clapping wildly, stamping, whistling, yelling.

'Well, that's all we've got time for now!' said the Doctor chirpily, straight to the camera. 'Goodnight. And happy Hallowe'en!'

The tinny voice in Corynne's ear said: '*And we're out.*'

The Doctor's smile suddenly fell. 'You all right?'

'Fine', said Dennis. 'Fine. You know, for a minute there, I really thought…' His face was a picture of misery.

'Dennis!' cried Corynne, racing towards him, finger pressed to her ear-piece. 'Clive's on the line. Breezy-TV's switchboard's gone into meltdown. We're a hit!'

Dennis frowned. 'But what about *Freaked Out?*'

He turned – but the Doctor was nowhere to be seen.

There was a sharp intake of breath from close by. Dennis and Corynne both swung round to find Simon gazing down at the cold, prone form of Preston Gilchrist.

'Well someone took it very seriously,' lisped Simon. 'I think Preston's scared hisself to death!'

THE END

Bennelong Point

WRITTEN BY **KEITH TEMPLE**   ILLUSTRATIONS BY **NEILL CAMERON**

'm opening my eyes. I guess I must have been asleep but something's not quite right and I can't put my finger on it. I'm feeling kind of weird. My head's all… fuzzy. I mean, I wake up every day and it's no big deal – why should it be? I'm sixteen, not ninety-six – I can afford to take going to sleep and expecting to wake up again the next morning for granted but I'm usually in my bed with the old familiar things around me, like the wardrobe with the broken door, the model planes hanging from the ceiling and all my books and records. Thing is, I'm not in my room. I'm on the floor somewhere. If I look to my right and left, the seats around me are fixed. There's a vibration too. I can feel it coursing down my back as I lie here, pinned to the floor. We're moving – travelling. Hang on! Pinned to the floor? What goes on here? I'm focussing now, I'm looking up and there's a guy in a suit above me. He's not just above me: he has his knee on my chest, making movement impossible. He's holding this pen thing with a blue light and he's shining it in my eyes. Maybe he's a doctor. Maybe I fainted or something.

Wish I could remember. Somehow, I can't. I'm thinking now that he probably works in a bank. Where I come from, the only guys who wear suits work in the bank. But where *do* I come from? I can't remember that either. It's a blank. Starting to feel scared now. I try to push the guy away because it's painful.

'Get your boney knee off me,' I manage to say.

The fella is grinning now and he's helping me to my feet. Oof! Dizzy. What a headache. At least I can look around properly. Hey! What do you know! I'm on a train. Whizzing through a barren landscape like a speeding bullet. There's nothing much to see. Desert, is it? Not sure. Why am I on a train? Once again, I don't know. I'm trying to remember. Nothing's coming to me – except for little things. Like my room, wherever that is. An image of a farm. Cattle. But it's all meaningless. It's like the inside of my head's a quarter-finished jigsaw puzzle. I can see little pieces of the picture but the rest's just an empty space. What's really frightening is, I don't know who I am. I don't even remember my name.

'All right, Harvey? You're going to be fine.'

That's the guy with the boney knees again. Harvey?
I'm called Harvey?

'Your memory will come back. Promise. Do you remember anything at all?'

I shake my head and ask him if he works in a bank. He doesn't. He's called the Doctor. So I guess he works in a medical centre. He tells me we're on a train, heading for Sydney. Why, I don't know.

'What if I say "Zalphon Mind Skippers"?' He's trying to jog my memory I suppose but it's not helping and I'm feeling like a drongo.

'No, mate.'

'Esperance?'

Now this is starting to ring a bell. Esperance. I'm remembering something...

He spins me around quickly and shouts, 'July 12th, 1979 – three days ago. Mean anything to you?'

Yes! It's all coming back. I'm in my bedroom. Looking out at the black night and the twinkling heavens, like I always do when I can't sleep. Three nights ago something different happened. The sky suddenly lit up. Orange, red and green glowing orbs rained down around the farm. Then there was the 'whoomph', 'whoomph', 'whoomph' of the sonic booms as whatever it was re-entered Earth's atmosphere. Hold on a minute!!!

'Skylab!' I yell. 'Skylab crashed back to Earth! That's when it all started!'

'Good lad,' says the Doctor. 'You're remembering.' He's slapping me on the back now. 'Few minutes, you'll be as right as rain'.

I sit down slowly as the events of the past few days, all the terrifying and wonderful images, start tumbling back into my consciousness. 'NASA's space station fell out of orbit and crashed on my house!' I manage to gasp.

'Sort of,' nods The Doctor.

'We've been invaded by aliens!'

The Doctor nods again. 'Looks like it.'

Real live aliens. Here in Australia. I put my head in my hands, feeling slightly sickened.

'And my name really is "Harvey"?'

'Oh yes!'

I close my eyes again. The headache isn't easing at all.

Three Days Earlier

Nothing exciting ever happened to me. I lived on a farm helping my dad with the cattle; I went to school, played a bit of footie, and watched TV. Life was routine. Esperance, my nearest town, was a quiet kind of place. Don't get me wrong, I loved it. It's where I grew up. It was full of happy memories for me. And after Mum died those happy memories became even more important to me but I wanted to experience the world beyond Esperance, Western Australia. That wasn't going to be possible while Dad needed me. The farm wasn't making a profit anymore. He'd had to let some of the lads go. He relied on me to help out.

That's when I got into stargazing. Peering through a telescope at the moon and the stars every night made me forget all my troubles and worries. When I heard the news that Skylab – the NASA space station, part spaceship, part windmill, whirling around the Earth – was due to fall out of orbit imminently and that it just might possibly crash somewhere in the Indian Ocean off the coast of Western Australia, I spent the evenings with one eye glued to my telescope. This was going to be the most exciting thing that happened to me ever. It didn't matter that the boffins were also forecasting it to come down in India or Canada, I just knew in my bones – Australia was where it would land.

Nobody, though, least of all me, expected the thing to almost flatten our farm. Which is exactly what happened in the early hours of July 12th. Dad was asleep, I could hear his snoring through the walls as I flipped the lens cap over my telescope and prepared to travel to the Land of Nod. The sky suddenly lit up like a blazing fire as bright balls of light rained down. It was as bright as day. The first sonic boom knocked me off my feet and my bedroom window shattered. Dad stumbled into my room telling me to get out quick! We ran out of the house, all the time looking up as tiny red hot objects slammed onto our corrugated roof. Dad yelled out in alarm as a larger fireball streaked over the rooftop and landed with a violent thud in the Bush beyond the farm.

'It's Skylab, Dad!' I shouted.

He grabbed me and we ran over to his battered old utility truck.

'Where are we going?'

'Whatever's just landed way over yonder looked pretty big. Might be worth something as salvage.' He had a point. Most of the debris landing on the house was charred and too small to be worth anything. Maybe the Americans and NASA would pay us to give them larger pieces of their space station back.

'Okay,' I said, 'let's give it a go.' And off we went, into the Bush.

Darkness had returned and everything was quiet by the time we parked up the ute and stumbled into the undergrowth but thankfully our torches cast a wide arc of light. We found the objects – for there were two – without much difficulty. They had fallen a few feet away from each other. One lay half-buried in an area of open ground. The other lay on its side at the foot of a tree on the edge of some scrub. Cylindrical in shape, metallic and charred, about the size of

an attaché case, they smouldered away, looking kind of dangerous. I noticed that the cylinder in the Bush was open at one end. Dad moved slowly towards it.

'Leave it Dad,' I whispered – not really knowing why. 'I don't like this.' Before I could figure out why I was feeling so unsettled we both stopped in our tracks.

Someone was moving in the Bush. We could hear a cracking sound as branches were pushed aside. The movement came nearer. We could hear heavy breathing. A section of bush parted but we continued to aim our torchlight with shaking hands.

We both laughed with relief as a kangaroo hopped out into the clearing.

Amusement quickly turned to horror though. I felt the hairs on the back of my neck standing up.

'Dad!' I said. 'Look at its eyes!'

Instead of the brown eyes we were used to, this animal was staring at us through glowing white sockets. It snarled violently, baring sharp fangs. Dad yelled and the creature backed away, disappearing into the Bush.

'Stay here!' he ordered and ran off into the undergrowth after it.

As I sat there, trying to work out if we'd accidentally discovered a new variety of marsupial, a strange noise reached my ears. It sounded like a rusty old engine. An old engine combined with a wheezing squeezebox. I shone my torch around, trying to locate the source of the sound but it proved impossible. What my torch beam did eventually show up though was the silhouette of a bloke. A tall thin fella in a brown stripey suit. No kidding. I didn't even have time to be scared because he bounded over to me all smiles and chatty as if we were old mates who'd just bumped into each other in the street.

'Hello,' he said in a Pommy voice. I think he was about to say more but then he saw the cylinders and started frowning.

'Oh dear. That's not good. One of them's opened up.'

'We found them first,' I said. 'Pieces of Skylab. We found them so they belong to us.'

The weird fella started tutting and pacing about.

'"Us", you say? Who else is here? Did they open the device?'

Before I could tell him, he kind of worked out the answer for himself because Dad stepped out into the clearing. I laughed. Not just because I was pleased to see him. Sometimes he can be a bit of a larrikin – a joker, playing daft tricks, that sort of thing. That's what I was laughing at.

'Dad, it's the middle of the night,' I said, 'why are you wearing sunglasses?'

He didn't answer. I don't even think he heard me. Instead he walked over to the buried cylinder, grabbed the upper section and pulled until the entire object was out of the ground. All the time the stranger kept watching him closely. Dad seemed not to notice him. He placed the cylinder in the ute and climbed in.

I called out, 'Hey! Wait for me!' He was already turning over the motor as I jumped in the cabin.

The fella in the suit ran alongside the van.

'He's not been completely absorbed yet,' he said. 'But it won't be long. Get away from him as soon as you can.'

Huh! I was right. The guy was after our salvage after all. Divide and conquer! That was his plan.

Tough cookie mister. Must think I was born yesterday!

Dad and I drove home in silence. Luckily for us the house was still standing when we got back, apart from a few holes in the tin roof and a one or two broken windows.

◄─◆─►

I didn't get much sleep that night – or what was left of the night. I had strange dreams about zombie kangaroos and men in brown suits.

When I went down to breakfast next morning, Dad was sitting at the kitchen table. Wearing his sunglasses. Turning on the transistor radio to listen to the news, I asked him to take his glasses off. He ignored me. Then the news started and I forgot about everything else.

The item about Skylab falling to Earth was interesting enough, but it was the last section of the bulletin which interested me. The *Sydney Morning Globe* was offering twenty thousand dollars to the person who could bring them the biggest piece of Skylab debris. Twenty thousand dollars! A fortune. Well, not quite. But it would solve some of our problems. We could pay off some of our debts. Build a new barn. I asked Dad what he thought. The unopened cylinder – the undamaged one – was fairly big, compared to the tiny bits and pieces we saw falling on the house. We could take it to Sydney – to the newspaper's head office.

Dad got all shirty and told me to forget about it. Mostly we discuss things, we rarely argue, but not this time. Dad wouldn't even listen to me. I tried to make him see sense. No luck. This wasn't like him. And what was with the sunglasses?

I turned away from him. His miserable mood and the sunglasses were really making me mad. Good job I looked out of the window when I did. The stranger was poking around the far barn and I didn't like it one bit. I knew what he was after.

⬡ ◇ ⬡

I checked out the barn. There was no sign of the stranger and the cylinders were where Dad had left them last night. On his workbench. I ran a hand over the intact device. It was still warm. The cylinders must have been glowing hot from re-entering the Earth's atmosphere when Dad first picked them up. How come he hadn't burned himself? I was still trying to work things out when I was suddenly knocked off my feet and sent sprawling along the floor. I looked up startled, thinking it must have been the thin guy, trying to get his grubby hands on my twenty thousand dollar space flotsam.

But it wasn't. It was Dad.

'Leave them alone!' he snarled.

'What's wrong with you? Why are you acting like this?' I howled. I was furious and was about to tell him exactly what I thought of him as I struggled to sit up, but my anger quickly vanished. For as he stepped towards me, the sunglasses slipped from the bridge of his nose and I found myself staring up at two brightly glowing white eyes.

'Dad!' I screamed. 'Dad! What's happened to you?'

An unearthly bellow emanated from somewhere within him and his face twisted into a snarl. His teeth were now fanged and sharp and he bared them as he crouched down ready to pounce. A split second later and I heard a loud buzzing, like hundreds of bees in a jar. The stranger stood in the doorway, pointing a pen-type thing with a blue light on the end at my Dad, who had started to shake and wail uncontrollably. I leaped to my feet.

'Stand away,' ordered the stranger.

I thought it best to do as he said – he had one of those 'don't mess with me, mate' expressions on his face.

Dad fell to the ground clutching his head. As I watched a bright green cloud of gas – or something that looked like gas, except it wasn't, because it was too thick and bright and shiny to be just gas – poured out of his ears and nose and mouth and hovered like a small cloud above him. The stranger leaped over to the intact cylinder, pointed his noisy blue torch thing over it, and what do you know? A panel in the side slid open and the cloud of green gas stuff – all of it – was sucked inside like chip fat smoke into an extractor fan.

The panel slid shut with a hiss. This was all very strange. But there wasn't time to think about strange things with my dad lying unconscious on the ground. I knelt down and shook him.

'He's going to be fine,' the stranger promised. 'I shocked the Zalphon out of his mind with a sonic blast.' He shook the cylinder. 'Bit of a tight fit in there but they won't get out. Phew!'

It was all gobbledegook as far as I was concerned. All I cared about was my dad. 'How do you know he'll be fine?' I asked.

'I'm the Doctor,' he replied. 'I know most things. Well, a lot of things. Well, some things. Well, one or two. And you are?'

'Harvey.'

'Nice to meet you, Harvey,' he said, then he knelt down beside me and felt Dad's pulse.

'Mind's still turning cartwheels but he'll get over it.'

He stood up and inspected the cylinder. 'You think these things are from Skylab, don't you?'

'I know they are,' I said. 'I saw it crash.'

The Doctor shook his head. 'Skylab fell out of its orbit last night and crashed to Earth,' he stated. 'But the lights in the sky? The explosions, the debris? That was something crashing *into* Skylab.'

I still had my suspicions. Was he trying to get his hands on my Skylab wreckage, nick it and claim the twenty thousand dollars? I wasn't sure. I asked him how he knew all this.

'I told you,' he grinned, 'I'm the Doctor. I was parked in orbit myself, watching it all happen.

'These,' he continued, indicating the cylinders, 'are escape pods. For a Zalphon scout ship. One pod for each passenger. The open pod was damaged on impact, allowing the Zalphon inside to escape and take over your dad.'

'Zalphon?' I asked. I was beginning to think this bloke might be a few kangaroos short of a full herd.

He nodded. 'Zalphons are gaseous-ectoplasmic organisms. Mind skippers. They travel the universe, feeding on brain energy and thought patterns. They're parasites. They take you over, absorb you, discard you and move on.'

This was getting ridiculous. I know I'd seen some pretty strange things recently, but aliens? Mind-absorbing green gas clouds? I don't think so. Something weird had certainly happened to Dad, that was

true. And as a result, I could only think of one thing – what if he didn't get better? We needed twenty thousand dollars more than ever. I had to get to Sydney to claim my reward. I had to get rid of this guy.

'Good on ya mate,' I said in a lighthearted sort of way. 'Well, you can be on your way now. Emergency over, eh?'

'Fraid not,' he said. 'There's a problem. You see the Zalphon ship that collided with Skylab – it was on its way from Earth. It was leaving the planet, which suggests they're here already. I've disabled the distress call signal on the escape pod. But you can bet back-up's on the way.'

The sound of a car door slamming made us both freeze. The Doctor put a finger to his lips and tiptoed to the door. He beckoned me over, asked if I knew the three men in suits who were on their way to the house. I didn't recognise them at all.

'Zalphons!' said the Doctor. 'They're wearing sunglasses.'

'This is Australia! Everybody wears sunglasses.'

Something peculiar happened as I spoke. The three men turned and looked in the direction of the barn and instead of walking up to the house they started to make their way over to us. I made a joke about them detecting our brain patterns and the Doctor nodded seriously. Then he came to life, slamming the barn door shut and commanding me to grab some bales of hay. He grabbed a few himself and started stacking them against the door as a barricade.

While he was doing all that I arrived at a decision – not that I mentioned anything to the Doctor. Making sure he wasn't watching me, I picked up the cylinder (I refused to call it an escape pod) containing the green cloudy stuff and ran to the back of the barn where I knew the clapboards were loose. It caused a bit of a disturbance and the Doctor looked around.

But it was too late. I crawled through the hole in the wall and before I knew it I was out in the open. As I ran and ran, I heard the Doctor's voice calling out after me.

'Harvey! No! Come back! *HARRR-VEEEEE!!!*'

The Doctor's helping me off the floor of the train and into a seat. Of course, I remember the Doctor. The man I was running away from. Things are coming back to me by the minute.

I glance across the carriage and notice the escape pod lying on a table. I have a sneaking suspicion about my memory loss – I think I know how it happened.

Outside the window, some houses flash by. Civilisation! My head's still aching but it's getting better. I breathe deeply and the Doctor smiles at me. I ask him where I am and how he found me. He tells me we're on a train. The Indian Pacific train, from Perth to Sydney. A journey of three days over more than four thousand miles of railway track. And it looks like it's almost over. We're on the outskirts of Sydney.

He starts to look all pleased with himself when he explains how he found me. He's a bit of a show pony, this Doctor fella. Likes to impress. He is good, though. After using his sonic screwdriver – the blue torch thing – to sort out those Zalphons who came snooping at the farm, he knew I'd be heading for Sydney – but by which method of transport? Hitching? Not a good idea. No guarantee I'd get a ride (spot on Doc, mate, my thoughts exactly). Aeroplane? Hardly. Too expensive (I only had five dollars in my pocket when I ran away). Coach (again too expensive). Which leaves… train. Also, prohibitive, cost wise but with better opportunities to stow away.

'It's like sharing a train cabin with Sherlock Holmes,' I laugh. The Doctor seems to like that. 'But what I want to know is, how come I ended up on the floor here with your knee on my chest and my memory full of holes?'

He sits me down, puts a hand on my shoulder. 'Nothing to worry about now. One of the Zalphons escaped from the pod and tried to absorb you.'

As soon as he's telling me this, it's all coming back to me –
I'm on the bus to Perth. Then I'm at the railway station, sneaking
on board the train to Sydney, hiding in bathrooms in corridors,
hugging the escape pod close to me all the time because it's
important. It's worth twenty thousand dollars.

I change bathrooms every few hours in order not to bring
suspicion upon myself. I walk up and down, to exercise my aching
legs, careful as I do so to avoid ticket inspectors and train staff.

The hours go by so slowly. The days too. And I wonder with a
stab of fear in my heart, if anyone has beaten me to the headquarters
of the *Globe*, handed over a piece of Skylab and claimed the reward.

Now I'm walking along, with the pod under my arm, trying
to look like an ordinary traveller on his way to the restaurant
car, hoping I can buy something decent with my remaining three
dollars. There are people all around me wearing sunglasses. Are they
Zalphons? Am I crazy to believe this Doctor fella?

I carry on through the train. The next carriage is empty except
for one fella, reading the *Sydney Morning Globe*. I look over as
I pass, trying to catch the headlines to see if the prize has been
claimed. I can only see his messy hair over the top of his newspaper.
I consider asking him if I could maybe take a peek.

''Scuse me…' I start to say, but
the guy holding up the paper
drops it and it's him. The
Doctor. Grinning away at me!

So he really *is* after me and
I bet it's to get his hands on
the prize money. He's about to
speak but there's a terrific bang, the
train lurches and we're both thrown
around the cabin as brakes squeal and
the passengers start to wail. The cylinder
shoots out from under my arm with the
impact and slams into the edge of a table.

'What happened?' I manage to say. I've hurt
my arm and I ache all over.

'Cattle on the track, I imagine. Happens
sometimes,' the Doctor replies. Trouble is he's not looking at me.
He's staring past me. I look around and a cloud of green ectoplasm
is curling towards me.

I want to run but I can't seem to move. Icy ectoplasmic fingers
stroke my face and I'm starting to forget everything. I'm cold
and empty...

◇ ◇ ◇

The Doctor's laughing as he tells me I was all staring white eyes
and blank zombie expression – but only for a few seconds – the
time it took for him to zap the escaped Zalphons out of my mind
with his sonic screwdriver (man, I love that sonic screwdriver!)
and lock them back in the pod.

My mind's a lot clearer now and I'm asking the Doctor some
important questions. What do the Zalphons want? And if they
really are planning on feeding off all our memories – turning the
human race into zombies – why is the Doctor helping me get this
pod thing to Sydney? It pains me to say this, considering it's worth
twenty grand, but I'm starting to think maybe we should destroy it.

But the Doctor's convinced we should take it to the *Sydney
Morning Globe*. I don't get it.

'I think you deserve the prize,' he says, 'and I also believe in
giving people what they want.'

I'm beginning to get to know him and I can see he's hiding something.
We're in Sydney now so it's too late to do anything about it.

◇ ◇ ◇

Outside the station, we make our way to the taxi rank. Loftus
Street's our destination – not far from the Opera House.

Before we can jump in the nearest cab, a van's roaring over
to us – all blacked out windows and squealing tyres. Two men
in black suits and sunglasses are jumping out. They're
clamping their sweaty hands over our mouths and bundling
us in the back. The Doctor's amazingly calm.

'Thanks for the lift' he says to the bloke sitting opposite us. Yeah – he's wearing sunglasses and he looks kind of familiar. I know who he is.

'You're Wade Johnson! Editor of the *Sydney Morning Globe*!'

'Well, he was,' says The Doctor. 'He's Zalphon Wade Johnson now!'

'Thank you for returning my associates,' says Zalphon Wade in a gravelly, alien-possessed kind of voice, and he grabs the escape pod from me.

'During their last bid for freedom, our fellow Zalphons managed to send a psychic alarm alerting us to their whereabouts.'

'Never mind that,' I say, 'what about my twenty thousand dollars?'

The Doctor taps my knee. 'Er, Harvey. There isn't any money. It was a ploy.'

I'm not massively understanding this so I let him carry on.

'What better way to ensure your missing "equipment" finds its way back to you if you can't find it yourself? Advertise a reward.'

It's all fitting together now and I'm not liking it because I'm starting to look like a galah – pretty stupid.

Zalphon Wade's talking to the Doctor now. None of it's making sense to me – something about being unable to read his thought patterns and the Doctor's muttering 'Time Lord' or something. I'm more interested in seeing where we're going, but of course the windows are blacked out.

'What happened with Skylab?' the Doctor's asking.

'An accident,' says Zalphon Wade. 'We were using the defunct space station to map the co-ordinates of every human on the planet as it circled the Earth. Our scout ship was extracting the last of the co-ordinate information when Skylab lost its orbit and collided with us.'

I'm interested now. 'Why do you want to know where we all are?'

The Doctor is adopting that smug Sherlock Holmes-y 'I-Know-It-All' expression again. 'You've been here for a few years,' he says to Zalphon Wade, 'but your plans to control and infect the Earth aren't going as fast as you'd like. If you knew the co-ordinates of every single person on the planet, you could just zoom into low orbit and zap a Zalphon into every human being on the globe. Presto – instant world domination!'

Zalphon Wade is nodding, and even though he's a zombie of sorts, he looks quite pleased with himself. 'A mothership big enough to carry an unimaginable army of Zalphon souls has been built.'

'What? Here in Sydney?' I say. Like I believe that!

'Once in orbit my army will swarm across the planet, infecting and absorbing all human life!' He lifts the cylinder off my knee. 'We have the final co-ordinates now. The countdown is ready!'

So now we're in a lift at the back of some building or other – the Zalphon thugs kept pushing our heads down, making it difficult to get our bearings as we stumbled out of the van – but if there's a spaceship in the middle of Sydney then I'm a cockatoo!

We're going up, up, up. And now the doors are opening onto this weird, futuristic, glowing room. It's like the bridge of a ship, with pyramid shaped control desks. At least I guess that's what they are.

I run over to the windows at the far side and look down onto a huge chamber below. There are thousands, maybe millions of opaque containers, like petrol barrels, all glowing green.

'The Zalphon Army,' mutters the Doctor.

We both watch as Zalphon Wade opens the hatch on the escape pod. Two fingers of green ectoplasmic gas stream out, whirl around the top of one of the pyramid control desks like swirling storm clouds, and disappear inside the mechanism.

The Doctor and me, we're staggering around now, because the floor and the walls are shaking. One of Zalphon Wade's thugs is

telling us the co-ordinates are in place and countdown has commenced. I'm about to ask the Doctor if he's got any plans but it's obvious he must have because he's taken off like a rocket himself, dashing around the room with his sonic screwdriver, waving it all over the place.

Zalphon Wade and his pals are trying to stop him, but then they're suddenly screaming and stumbling, green gas pouring out of them.

The Doctor's shouting above the noise of the giant rocket engines somewhere far below. 'Get them into the lift!'

We stagger with Wade and his goons into the lift, and before we know it, it's headed for ground level.

'What did you do?' I ask. The roaring around us is unbearable now.
'Reset the coordinates. For Antarctica.'

I don't like the sound of that. 'I don't want them anywhere near my planet, Doctor. They'll just come back!'

The Doctor's grinning that all-knowing grin again. 'No they won't. Why do you think they chose Australia as their base? Zalphons and Zalphon technology – they can't stand extreme cold. Ectoplasm turns to ice crystals. So no more Zalphons!'

He's really smart, this Doctor Whoever-He-Is.

Bang! The lift's stopping at ground level with a creaking, grating noise, only just audible above the din of the engines. Wade and his mates – who aren't Zalphons anymore, just groggy humans – are on their feet and running out into the daylight, away from the mothership. I'm running too but I want to look back and see what this spaceship is. A spaceship in the middle of Sydney?

I shield my eyes and look up at the familiar white shapes of the structure above. I'm taking in the sail-like arches. I'm looking at the Sydney Opera House!

But not for long. We all fall to the ground as rocket engines, buried below the surface, ignite – and the entire opera house takes off into the sky. The Doctor is laughing and whooping. Me? I'm still in shock. Sydney Opera House is a spaceship?! Who knew? Wade and his pals are also stuck for words. In fact, their jaws are somewhere around their feet.

Suddenly the Doctor's up and running again. 'Come on!' he yells.
'What's the rush?' I ask.

'Do you want to tell people what's happened to the opera house? Might be a bit difficult!'

I'm twenty thousand dollars down but I suddenly realise – I know I way to make some cash. Dad and me, maybe we can rebuild the barn, get the farm up and running again after all. I turn to Wade Johnson, editor of the *Sydney Morning Globe,* who is still lying at my feet, looking dazed and confused.

'Wade,' I say, 'have I got the story of the century for you!'

I look around. Hordes of people are hurrying towards the gaping hole in the ground at Bennelong Point where the opera house used to stand. They're coming towards us, screaming, yelling. Out of the corner of my eye I catch sight of one man going against the crowd, fighting his way through the masses, anxious to distance himself. He waves at me without looking back.

'See you, Doctor!' I holler. 'Nice knowing you!' But I don't think he's heard me and pretty soon he's lost in the throng.

Wade's on his feet, pulling out a notebook.

'Yeah,' I say, 'the story's all yours. An exclusive! And it'll only cost you twenty thousand dollars...'

THE END

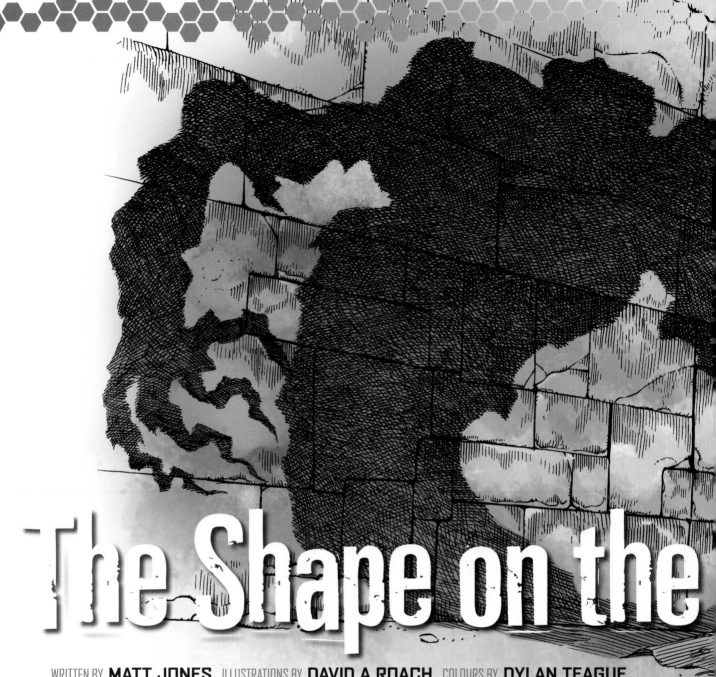

The Shape on the

WRITTEN BY **MATT JONES**   ILLUSTRATIONS BY **DAVID A ROACH**   COLOURS BY **DYLAN TEAGUE**

'He's back,' Rosie whispered as she climbed into Lola's bed. 'The man on the chair, he's come back!'

Lola sighed and put her arm around her little sister, pulling her under the thin blanket that smelt of damp. 'Don't be silly, Rosie, it's just a pile of clothes.'

'You look!'

Lola put her finger to her lips. 'Ssh, you'll wake the others.' But if the chorus of snores were to be trusted, none of the other girls in the dormitory had been woken by Rosie's exclamation.

Lola peered across the room at the rotten, crumbling armchair where the girls threw their scratchy uniforms every night before hurrying across the cold stone floor to their straw beds.

Silhouetted against the barred window, the pile of abandoned dresses did look a little like a malformed, shapeless man, slumped in the chair as if the worse for gin or despair. If she fancied, Lola could make out a head, shoulders and arms...

She shivered. 'It's nothing to be scared of,' she told her little sister. 'Monsters aren't real. They live only in the pages of stories.'

'You promise?' Rosie whispered, and cuddled in tight.

'I promise,' Lola said.

Which was when the shape on the chair, which couldn't possibly be anything other than a pile of dresses, came alive and heaved itself to its feet!

It was all Lola could do not to scream in terror. The shapeless, shifting monster lurched a few steps towards her, and then paused, swaying to and fro.

It made a familiar sound. It took Lola a moment to realise that it was sniffing the air! Was it trying to get their scent?

'But if there are no monsters in real life, where do the monsters in stories–' Rosie started to say.

Lola clamped a hand over her little sister's mouth. 'You're going to have to be very quiet,' she whispered in Rosie's ear.

Lola felt Rosie wriggle in her grip. Before Lola could stop her, Rosie had seen the monster from her nightmares come to life – and she screamed!

The monster spun around at the sound and charged towards them, a shifting mass of material, animated by something Lola could not begin to imagine.

She grabbed Rosie's hand and made a mad dash for the dormitory doors, pulling her sister along behind her like a doll.

The door was locked. Lola's heart was thundering in her chest. She heard the soft sound of material being dragged across the stone floor and whirled around to discover that the monster was upon them.

The creature grabbed hold of Rosie and tried to carry her off, but instinctively Lola clung to Rosie's arms. Rosie yelped as the monster pulled her feet and she ended up in a tug of war between them.

Chair

Despite being made of clothes, the monster was incredibly strong. Lola felt herself being pulled forward, almost off her feet. A gaping mouth appeared in the monster's head and it started to swallow Rosie, inch by inch.

'Lola!' Rosie yelled in terror. 'Don't let it eat me!'

Lola pulled on Rosie's arms as hard as she could, but she knew that she was no match for the shapeless, shifting man. Rosie was going to be eaten and there was nothing she could do to stop it!

Just as she lost her footing and lurched forward, she felt someone grab hold of her feet. 'It's alright, I've got you!' a new voice said.

A man she had never seen before was there, holding tightly onto her feet with one hand and the doorknob with the other. The man grinned. 'Hello,' he shouted, 'I'm the Doctor! How do you do?' Lola was too surprised to answer. She was sure the door had been locked.

The Doctor pulled on Lola's feet, Lola pulled on Rosie's arms and slowly Rosie's feet emerged out of the monster's gaping mouth.

Lola was relieved to see Rosie's feet were quite unharmed from their experience inside the monster. And then, just when it looked like the misshapen creature would be forced to let Rosie go, the door to the dormitory opened without warning, the Doctor lost his grip on the doorknob, unbalancing Lola who lost her grip on Rosie, who tumbled towards the shapeless monstrous thing which seized its moment and swallowed her whole!

'What, by all the Saints in Heaven, is going on?' Mrs Hatchet demanded, standing in the doorway, one hand on the doorknob and the other clutching a quart of gin.

Lola ignored her. 'Rosie!' she cried, but the monster had vanished taking Rosie with it. All that remained were the dresses, fluttering lifelessly to the floor.

From behind Lola came Mrs Hatchet's shrill, slurred voice. 'What do you think you're doing in my orphanage? Make one move towards me and I'll have the full weight of the law down upon you!'

The Doctor didn't seem the least intimidated by Mrs Hatchet. 'How do you do? I'm Doctor John Smith from–'

'You could be King William for all I care! And even if you were, you've no right to be in a dormitory for young girls.'

'Surprise inspection,' the Doctor said, pulling out a wallet and flipping it open to reveal his credentials.

And now she didn't even have her. The Doctor knelt down so that he was at eye level with Lola. 'It's alright, we'll find her,' he said, with such certainty that Lola found she had no choice but to believe him. 'I promise you. We'll find your sister.'

'Little Rosie's not the first to go missing,' Agatha the kitchen maid muttered nervously as she stirred an enormous saucepan of gruel. 'Lots of girls have disappeared over the years. Mrs Hatchet tells the trustees that they run away. But it's not true.'

'How can you be sure?' the Doctor asked.

Agatha nervously peered at the Doctor and Lola over the steaming pan of foul smelling food. 'Because you can hear them in the walls, crying.'

'In the walls? Really?' The Doctor produced a stethoscope from his pocket, stuck the ear pieces in his ears and pressed the other end up against the cold stone walls of the kitchen.

'Staff won't stay,' Agatha continued. 'It's not just disappearing girls. Things move that have no business moving. Last year a lass was attacked by a mangle. Lost two fingers and half her thumb! A mangle! It's not right!'

'So why do you stay, Agatha?' the Doctor asked, still listening at the wall.

'I was born here, wasn't I? It's all I've known. If I wasn't more scared of the outside world, I'd be off like a shot.'

'Well you're right that the girls haven't run away,' the Doctor said and nodded Lola over to the wall. 'Lola, listen to this.'

Lola took the stethoscope. At first she couldn't hear anything, and then very slowly she became aware of cries, very faint as if far away.

'The Crabtree Trust always conducts them before awarding grants.'

'Grants?' Mrs Hatchet asked. 'Did you say grants?' She made a show of examining the Doctor's credentials whilst flipping the lid of her gin bottle closed and pocketing it, all in one smooth movement.

'Oh yes, we always conduct the most thorough investigations before any monies exchange hands. I'll have to search... I mean *inspect* the facility from top to bottom.'

'Oh of course, no problem at all. My late husband built this place up from scratch. A wonderful man! I have nothing to hide.'

'Marvellous. Just one thing, I'll need a guide. I work better with an assistant.' The Doctor glanced over at Lola and winked hugely.

Lola had never met anyone quite like the Doctor before. He moved quickly through the orphanage, examining everything, endlessly asking her questions. He only paused when she explained how she and Rosie had come to be here. How her explorer parents had been lost at sea on their way home from Egypt, and how Rosie was all Lola had left in the world.

Girls' voices. Some were calling out for their mothers and fathers, others just howled in fear and despair.

One voice stood out, closer and louder than the others. '*Lola! Lola!*' It was Rosie.

'That's my sister! What's she doing in the wall!?'

'What indeed?' the Doctor muttered, peering thoughtfully at the huge stone bricks. 'And what a wall it is. There's a seam of crystal in the rock. Green crystal. I've seen something like it before, if only I could remember where. Or when for that matter.'

'I'd better be getting on,' Agatha said. 'The furnace won't feed itself.' She went to pick up a basketful of coal but her hands were shaking so much that she dropped it, sending black lumps rolling across the kitchen floor.

'What are you so scared of?' the Doctor asked her gently.

'Yesterday, I went down to the cellar to feed the furnace and... and it tried to bite me!' Agatha said, tears pricking at her eyes.

'Why don't you let me sort it out, Agatha?' the Doctor said, patting the scared maid on the shoulder. He turned to Lola. 'A furnace that bites! We don't want to miss that. What do you say?'

Lola didn't say anything. Her throat had become so dry she couldn't speak at all. Behind the Doctor, an angry orange glow was starting to fill the doorway to the cellar. The flickering fiery light was getting brighter and brighter. She could hear a clanking and hissing as *something* made its way up the stairs towards them.

'Everyone up on the table!' the Doctor shouted, grabbing hold of Lola's hands and lifting her up off the floor.

Suddenly the furnace scuttled around the door like a crab. It was so wide that it chipped chunks of stone from the doorway as it smashed its way into the kitchen. It was made of a heavy, dark metal, like iron. Fire burned from two glass windows which looked for all the world like eyes. Below them was a wide grill that dropped open and snapped closed with a vicious clang.

'Our Father who art in heaven–' Agatha started, palms together and eyes closed.

The Doctor whirled around at the sound of her voice. 'What do you think you're doing?' he shouted. 'Get up here!' But Agatha only sank to her knees and repeated the prayer with a desperate fervour.

The furnace seemed to sense its victim in the room, and Lola could've sworn that its wide grill curled up at the corners in an evil grin. 'Do something, Doctor!' she cried.

The Doctor grabbed hold of the washing line which hung above the kitchen table, and leaned out to reach for Agatha. 'Take my hand!' he demanded. But Agatha didn't seem to hear him.

There was the terrible scraping of metal on stone as the furnace pounced, opened its grill wide – and young Agatha was no more.

'Stay behind me!' the Doctor ordered Lola, as the furnace circled the table. He took out a small silver

pen-like object from his pocket and pointed it at the knot which held the washing line to the far wall. With a snap, the line came free and the Doctor quickly fashioned himself a lasso.

'I was the Kansas Rodeo Champion three years running, 1804, 1840, 1852,' the Doctor boasted, twirling the lasso over his head.

'That's not three years running,' Lola said, despite her fear.

'It was for me,' the Doctor replied, and threw the lasso across the room, far over the hissing furnace.

'You missed!' screamed Lola.

The Doctor looked her right in the eye and smiled. 'I never miss.'

Lola turned to see that the Doctor had actually lassoed poor Agatha's pan of steaming gruel. Waiting for the furnace to place itself between the table and the pan, the Doctor pulled hard on his makeshift lasso, tipping the pan from the stove, and showering the furnace in gallons of foul-smelling porridge.

Steam hissed from the furnace which sank to the ground, the fire in its eyes dying until it was a harmless, inanimate object once more.

'Poor Agatha,' said Lola, wiping away a tear. 'She never got to leave this horrible place.'

'Come on,' the Doctor said grimly. 'Let's find your sister.'

Lola held tightly to the Doctor's hand as they made their way slowly down the cellar stairs. The Doctor kept asking her questions about her old life before she came to the orphanage. Where had she gone to school? What had her friends been like? Where had she and Rosie lived?

Lola realised that the Doctor was trying to take her mind off the fact that she was exploring a dark, dank cellar where even the most innocent objects could come alive and attack you. She found herself wondering if the Doctor ever got scared. If he did, he didn't show it.

'What was that?' the Doctor asked.

Lola stared into the impenetrable darkness. 'I don't hear anything,' she started to say, then paused. There were children's voices, just like before. One voice was louder than the others, a voice she knew very well indeed.

'Rosie!' Lola shouted, 'I'm coming!'

Without thinking, she snatched the candle from the Doctor's hand and ran into the darkness to find her sister.

'Lola, wait!' the Doctor cried, but Lola didn't stop. Rosie was nearby – she had to find her.

The light from the candle revealed a door standing ajar at the end of a corridor. Lola pushed open the door and, calling her sister's name, ran through.

The door slammed shut behind her. The candle flickered and died. Lola was alone in the dark.

The Doctor ran blindly through the darkness, slamming headlong into a wall.

'Lola!' he shouted, and urgently began feeling for the door he had heard slam closed. It had gone, completely vanished. 'That's impossible,' he murmured to himself. But then he'd seen several impossible things since he had arrived at the orphanage.

'Lola, don't worry!' he shouted, not knowing if the little girl could hear. 'Stay where you are, I'm coming to find you!'

He felt along the wall, until he met the corner and set off again. But within a metre he had met another corner. That can't be right, he thought.

He stretched his arms out in all directions and discovered that his fingers could reach all four walls. The corridor had shrunk to the size of a cell.

And it was still shrinking! He could feel the stone walls moving closer on every side. The room was no longer the size of a cell, it had reduced to the size of a telephone box! If it carried on like this it was going to crush him!

The Doctor braced his arms against the walls, but try as he might they kept coming. He put his back against one of the walls, lifted his feet off the floor and desperately tried to hold off the oncoming wall, but when he felt his knees bang against his chin, he was forced to stand upright.

The walls closed in on all sides until he could feel them against his chest and back. He took one last desperate breath and waited for the inevitable.

After a moment, the Doctor exhaled. He was still alive! The walls had stopped. He was now standing in a coffin-sized space, his face so close to the walls that he could see the flecks of green crystal glowing softly in the dark stone.

He was still alive, but completely trapped. He wriggled his sonic screwdriver out of his pocket and tested the depth of the walls on all sides. According to his scan, the walls were forty metres deep. There was no way he was going to be able to dig his way out.

Is this how it ends? he wondered to himself. Eventually he would run out of air and suffocate. He'd regenerate, of course, but he'd only run out of air again, regenerate, suffocate, regenerate and on and on until he ran out of lives. How many did he have left? He couldn't remember.

'Well if you've gotta go, you've gotta go,' the Doctor whispered to reassure himself.

And then his hearts sank. He'd promised Lola that he would find her sister. He felt a sudden wave of anger and pushed helplessly against the cold walls.

He was going to let her down. That poor girl was lost alone in the darkness facing who knows what. And he wasn't there to help her.

He was always making promises – to get people home, to chase the monsters away, to save the world. He always knew deep down he shouldn't, that one day he might make a promise he couldn't keep.

The Doctor felt an emotion he wasn't familiar with at all: despair. It crept into his bones as he faced his worst fears.

The crystal in the stone walls seemed to respond to his hopelessness, bathing his face with an eerie emerald light which seemed to grow brighter the more despondent he felt.

'Hang on,' the Doctor said to himself. 'It *is* getting brighter. How is that possible?'

It was true. The crystal in the stone walls was now shining brightly. The Doctor broke into a massive grin as he finally remembered what the crystal was.

And he knew exactly what to do.

'Doctor?' Lola whispered. 'Where are you?'

Lola didn't like to admit it, but she was scared of the dark. It was easier to face when Rosie was there, because then Lola had someone to be brave for. Lola found herself missing Rosie desperately.

Like all sisters, they hadn't always got on. In the old days, Lola would quickly tire of playing games with Rosie that she herself had long since grown out of. But after they had come to the orphanage, things had changed. Now Lola would have given anything to play with Rosie again.

But Rosie was gone. And now she had lost the Doctor too.

Lola swallowed. There was something else. Something moving in the dark. Lola couldn't see anything, but she could hear it. She could hear it *breathing*. It was behind her and getting louder – which meant it was getting *nearer,* didn't it?

Something slithered and slid towards her in the darkness,

Lola opened her mouth to scream when suddenly the walls shone with a brilliant white light, a circle of huge stone bricks shuddered and then slid out of the wall, floating in the air around her!

The Doctor popped his head through the hole.

'Doctor!' Lola exclaimed, never more pleased to see anyone.

'*Allons-y!*' the Doctor yelled cheerfully, grabbed Lola's hand and pulled her to safety.

'I knew I'd seen that crystal somewhere before. It's Lucidian!' The Doctor was talking enthusiastically as he hurried through the corridors of the orphanage. 'Of course, you wouldn't have heard of the Lucidians. How could you? Before your time. Oh you would have loved them! Their crystalline stardrives actually magnified their cognitive-affective functioning.'

Lola didn't understand a word the Doctor had said. 'What's a stardrive?'

'Oh!' The Doctor came to an abrupt stop. 'Yes, er, right. Sorry, forgot where I was. Or when I was. 1852. Right, how best to put this?' He knelt down in front of Lola. 'The Lucidians came from another place, far away.'

'Like Egypt?'

'Bit further. Well, actually, quite a bit further. They were explorers, very special explorers. They built sailing ships that could fly between the stars.

'They flew in the heavens!' Lola gasped with excitement.

'They did!' the Doctor grinned, loving her enthusiasm. 'They really did. But because there's no wind between the stars, they made magic crystals which magnified their feelings, and they filled the ship's sails with their simple desire to explore. They literally flew by hope and wonder!'

'And they built the orphanage?'

'Ah, no, the Lucidian civilisation was far from here and long gone. The stone that was used to build the orphanage must have come from a quarry where one of their ships landed, or more likely crashed. But the crystal in the stone is resonating with our emotions, magnifying them, reflecting them.'

'So all we have to do is not feel scared and then our fears won't come alive?'

'Exactly! But the interesting question is, what was making you scared in the first place? Or, to be more precise, who?'

Mrs Hatchet had promised herself that she wouldn't have another drink until after Doctor Smith had completed his inspection and the grant was a done deal. So how was the bottle almost empty? It had been half full when she'd returned to her parlour.

Her Albert would never have allowed her to drink so much, and she had never had an appetite for it when he was alive. But he was gone, worn out running around after those girls. No wonder his heart had given out. He'd sacrificed any chance of a long life and a happy retirement for them. And did those brats show any gratitude? Not one jot.

A wave of bitterness rose up in her throat, and she washed it back down with another gin. Well why not? Albert wasn't here to see; she could drink all she liked. There was no-one here to care.

'Good evening, Mrs Hatchet.'

Doctor Smith was in the doorway with that new girl, the posh one, who looked down her nose at her.

'There you are, Doctor Smith.' Mrs Hatchet struggled a little unsteadily to her feet. The room swum around her and she had to blink it back into focus. 'I trust everything is to your satisfaction. I think you'll find I run a tight ship. The Trust's monies would be put to good use here.'

'What? Oh, the grant. I'm afraid not, Mrs Hatchet. That's out of the question.'

'I've been found wanting, have I? Not good enough? How so?'

'Well, where to begin?' the Doctor said. 'There's the terrible atmosphere for starters. You're unhappy, so you scare the children. They become withdrawn, which you take to mean they're ungrateful, which only makes you unhappier still. It's a vicious circle, and one that's only going to get worse.'

'How dare you presume to judge me!' Mrs Hatchet snapped, feeling simultaneously indignant at this impertinence and horribly exposed by the truth of his words.

'Calm down,' the Doctor urged, glancing at the walls around them. 'Let's not let our feelings run away with themselves.'

'Don't you tell me what to do! Not in my own house.' Mrs Hatchet could feel anger coursing through her veins. It felt good. Anything felt better than the constant ache of Albert's absence.

'You must stop resenting the children, Mrs Hatchet,' the Doctor implored. 'Your feelings are sending them away, banishing them into the very stones of the building. You have to want them to come back.'

'Ha! Those evil imps drove my Albert into an early grave. Why should I want them back?'

'If you won't bring them back, then I will,' the Doctor said.

'My Albert built this place up from nothing. I'm not having some self-righteous philanthropist telling me what to do in this house!'

Perhaps it was the gin, but the room seemed to be getting brighter. The walls lit up from within. Mrs Hatchet thought she was probably imagining it. One thing she was not imagining was that the angrier she got, the better she felt. It was time someone put that smug Doctor in his place.

Lola peered at Mrs Hatchet from behind the Doctor's legs. It wasn't just the tatty parlour that was glowing green. Mrs Hatchet was starting to glow as well, her eyes burning with the same eerie light. As she ranted and raved at the Doctor, the strange crystal in the walls pulsed in time with her words.

The room was filled up with so much bitterness and resentment that Lola could almost taste it on her tongue. She had never understood why Mrs Hatchet chose to run an orphanage if she hated children so much. If it really was the old woman's hatred that had been responsible for sending Rosie away, how was the Doctor going to be able to bring her back?

Lola looked up at the Doctor. He didn't appear to be listening to Mrs Hatchet. His eyes were closed, and a frown cut across his forehead, as if he were concentrating very hard.

The seams of crystal in the flagstones beneath the Doctor's feet started to change colour. Where they had been an eerie emerald, they were now starting to shine with a clear white light.

The light spread through the seams in the stone walls, and with it came a new emotion. Lola felt it all around her. It was the Doctor's bravery; he wasn't scared of Mrs Hatchet. Experiencing the Doctor's feelings in the room around her made Lola herself a little less frightened.

The Doctor opened his eyes and looked at Mrs Hatchet, who wilted under his gaze, and stumbled drunkenly back a step. 'You said your husband built this place up from scratch. He must've loved children. What would he have thought of you?'

Lola realised immediately that it was the wrong thing to say. Mrs Hatchet's face filled with fury. She pulled herself to her full height and screamed at the Doctor, 'Don't you dare bring him into this! You're not worthy to speak his name!'

An explosion of angry emotion burst out of Mrs Hatchet and slammed into the Doctor knocking him off his feet. Every resentment, every moment of self-pity she'd ever indulged, all her indignation at Albert's untimely death tore into the Doctor and he yelled in pain.

Lola ran to where the Doctor lay sprawled on the floor. His eyes were closed. Lola couldn't tell if he was breathing.

'Doctor!' Lola called out, shaking him. The Doctor wouldn't stir. But if the Doctor failed, if he died, then Lola would never see Rosie again! Tears brimmed in Lola's eyes; she had never felt so alone.

'Oh Albert,' Lola heard Mrs Hatchet cry into the air, 'how could you go and leave me?'

The terrible pain Lola felt at having lost Rosie forever made her understand exactly how Mrs Hatchet was feeling. The cruelty of losing the one person you had left – the person who was there just for you.

Lola turned to face the old woman who was glowing so brightly that she was barely recognisable.

Lola ran to Mrs Hatchet and flung her arms around her. 'I know just how you must feel!' Lola sobbed.

Mrs Hatchet looked down at Lola in surprise. Such was the sincerity on Lola's tear-stained face that Mrs Hatchet realised that Lola meant every word.

And for a moment, for a tiny moment, Mrs Hatchet didn't feel alone.

The room lit up with pure white light! Lola saw children's faces appear in the stone bricks. The walls became insubstantial and the missing children climbed down into the parlour! Laughing with the excitement and relief at being free, they charged through the orphanage looking for their brothers, sisters and friends.

Lola gently eased Mrs Hatchet into an armchair and went in search of her sister. She found her climbing out of a painting above the fireplace in the hall.

'Lola!' Rosie shouted and jumped from the mantelpiece into her arms. 'I knew you'd find me!' Rosie cried. 'I never doubted it, not for a moment.'

Lola didn't say anything. She just held her sister tightly and made a silent promise that she would never lose her again.

'It's time to say goodbye,' the Doctor told Lola and Rosie the next morning. He led them to a quiet corridor where someone had put a big blue box that Lola had never seen before.

'But where are you going?' Lola asked. 'Can't you take us with you?'

'I can't do that, Lola,' the Doctor said. 'Mrs Hatchet is going to need all your compassion to prevent her becoming bitter again. And she's going to need your help to look after so many children.

'In fact,' the Doctor added, a small smile creeping across his face, 'she's going to need rather a lot of help. So I, er, found us some new recruits...'

The Doctor fished out a key, unlocked the tall blue box and opened the door. Two people stepped out. People Lola

thought she would never see again. They were soaked to the skin and smelt of the sea.

For a moment Lola just stared, too scared to believe that they were real. Then she recognised the kindness in the woman's green eyes and the warmth in the man's easy smile and she knew it was really them.

It was her mother and father!

'I'm breaking all kinds of laws of time and space...' the Doctor started and then trailed off. No-one was paying him the least attention. The two girls had thrown their arms around their parents and were laughing and talking and crying all at the same time.

The Doctor watched as Lola and Rosie's joy at being reunited with their parents spread through the orphanage. The Lucidian crystal in the stone walls began to shine with a warm orange glow.

The Doctor looked in wonder as the building itself started to change. Its cruel spires softened into rounded domes, the narrow windows widened, as sunlight streamed through them chasing the shadows out of the corners.

With one last look at the girl whose bravery had let him keep his promise, the Doctor slipped into the TARDIS and was gone.

THE END

Knock Knock!

WRITTEN BY **PAUL MAGRS**   ILLUSTRATIONS BY **ADRIAN SALMON**

Mary and her young man were out late at the music hall. Afterwards, Tommy wanted a swift half down the pub. Now here they were, having a quick kiss and a cuddle in an alley nowhere near the big house in Beaton Square where Mary lived and worked.

'Mr Scoggins will go spare,' she protested.

Tommy just laughed.

Scoggins was the fierce butler in the big house. He kept a beady eye on who came and went by the servants' door. If you came tripping in late, he'd give you a right tongue-lashing.

'I have to be up at four, Tommy,' Mary sighed. 'I'm in the laundry tomorrow.'

Mary dreamed of one day running away. But where? And how? Tommy didn't have any money. There'd be no escape with him. No future in being with him, really. Best just have a bit of fun while she could. And knickers to old Cook and Mr Scoggins and everyone who told her what she should and shouldn't do.

Tommy realised that Mary wasn't kissing him with her full concentration. 'Where've you gone, sweetheart?'

She was looking up at the stars. The moonlight was bright in the alley. She just felt a bit strange this evening. Like something different was about to happen...

'Come through here.' Tommy found an opening in the fence. They could have a bit of privacy in the dark for a few moments.

Mary ducked after him, looking around at the bulky shapes that surrounded them in the gloom. 'Is this some kind of junkyard?'

'Who cares?'

Mary smelled varnish and paint. She saw that the yard was filled with doors. Hundreds of them were leaning like dominoes against each other.

'Ooh, it's a bit creepy. All these doors that don't go anywhere.' She peered at the intricate mouldings.

'Ignore them.' Tommy drew her to him and she found that they were leaning up against one of the doors. What if they set the whole lot tumbling down?

Something behind them gave a loud click.

'Tommy..?!' Mary realised with a jolt that the door he was leaning on had somehow sprung open. Tommy was staggering backwards with a look of alarm in his eyes. Now he was falling through the door itself...

He cried out in shock. The doorway was fully open now, revealing a scintillating darkness beyond. She saw Tommy's fingers scrabbling for purchase. For a moment he clung to the threshold. He called her name once...

Tommy was sucked into the great nothingness beyond the Door. Then he was gone. The Door slammed sharply.

Mary sobbed, staggering backwards. The yard was silent again.

She knew she had to get out of this weird place. What could she tell the police, though? They'd broken into where they shouldn't have. Mary scrambled through the hole in the fence, her mind buzzing.

Out in the alleyway she heard a weird noise. A wheezing noise horribly reminiscent of Cook snoring in the next bedroom in the servants' attic.

Mary watched, dumbstruck, as a blue box manifested itself. My God, the police were quick on the scene these days!

She hid in the shadows as one of the box's doors (more doors!) sprang open and a youngish man in a blue suit sprang out. His hair was just about standing on end as if with an electrical charge. He had the most amazingly intent gaze Mary had ever seen, with his eyebrows crooked into a questioning scowl as he peered round at his new environment.

Mary's heart was racing. Oh, help, what was this? Was he really from the police? Some secret kind, who could appear in a flash? Or was this strange man part of the same demonic force that had spirited Tommy away?

Mary wasn't going to wait to find out. She flung herself out of the shadows and fled for her life.

The quizzical man in the blue striped suit whipped his head round. Too late to catch up with her, though.

Mary ran all the way back to 256 Beaton Square. She stumbled down the familiar stairs to the servants' back door.

As she fiddled with her key she glanced up to see the butler's fierce eye magnified in his spyhole. Glaring down at her. She was caught – again!

The door flew open and Scoggins – standing there in his pyjamas – started scolding her. But Mary didn't care. She was glad to be back in the closest thing she had to a home. She broke down in tears and the grumpy butler had to catch her.

'Goodness me, girl,' he gasped. 'Whatever's the matter with you?'

That girl was definitely spooked, thought the Doctor. She'd run off before he could ask her a single question. Should he have run after? Naaaah. Whatever she was fleeing was still here. Still knocking about here, somewhere…

The Doctor padded around in the darkness. Squeaking. He could definitely hear squeaking. Giant mice? Rats? No, more mechanical than that. Squeeeek. Like hinges. Rusty castors…

He was being watched, he knew. He'd draw them out. He'd make them show themselves. He decided to take a brisk walk along the moonlit Thames. All the while he knew that there was something shadowy, dogging his every step. The Doctor wasn't easily scared. By walking about brazenly, he was announcing his presence to whoever it was that shouldn't be here.

The squeak-squeak-squeak at his heels was soon getting on his nerves. He swung round and shouted under the dank bridge: 'Why don't we stop mucking about? I can probably help, you know. What are you, caught in the wrong time? I know you're here somewhere. My ship detected you in this time zone. Is this really where you want to be? Tell the nice Doctor, eh?'

Whoever was slinking in the dark made no reply. Maybe, the Doctor mused, he was so used to skulking alien interlopers that he was now seeing them everywhere. He tried the word out under his breath, liking its sound: interloper. Were they called that because they went loping about? He'd have to ask, if he ever met them…

He hurried back to the brick archway. There. Was that dooorway there before? He wasn't sure. He gave the strangely ornate door a quick blast of his sonic. Couldn't touch it.

Why would a door be there, in amongst the bill posters and the green slime? Where would it lead? Nowhere very nice, he was sure.

Knock knock. The Doctor rapped hard and listened, frowning. He knocked again. He rattled the letterbox. 'Shop!' No answer. He bent to peer through the letterbox. 'C'mon! I'm hanging about out here!'

Aha! A swirling vortex of pink and purple lay beyond. Not what you might expect. He blinked and looked again. No, he hadn't imagined it. There was some kind of surreal nightmare dimension right behind this door. Rii-iii-ght.

Creeeak. He looked around sharply. Squueeeaaakkk.

There, at the end of the tunnel, was another of his pursuers.

The creature's silhouette was tall and oblong in shape. Incredibly thin. Squeaking on castors. The Doctor shook his head and rubbed his eyes incredulously.

'Hang on a bit. You're a door.'

He rubbed his eyes again.

'You're a perambulating wooden door. A living door!' He grinned broadly. 'Now, that's amazing. That's just brilliant! I've never met a walking door before... Ah-ah! Don't go!'

But the door was already slipping away on its tiny, speedy wheels. The Doctor boggled for a moment and then gave chase.

No use. He'd lost it. Chasing doors in Edwardian London? Was this what happened when he was left on his own, the Doctor wondered. But it was a door! A door going about of its own accord!

When he turned back into the tunnel he found that the first door was gone. The wall was flat and featureless apart from the torn posters.

That was a bit annoying.

Now it was like he'd just imagined the whole thing. Not a door in sight!

But at least he was right, he consoled himself. There was something peculiar in this place and time.

Something, some alien evil, was afoot.

Or was it... ajar?

Nothing was running as smoothly as it ought at number 256 Beaton Square. The household of His Majesty's Government's Home Secretary, the Right Hon Jeffrey Fairbairn was staffed by a smoothly-running unit of servants drilled with military precision by Mr Scoggins the butler.

But today there was an unfamiliar buzz of excitement. One of the serving girls had heard the family upstairs talking at breakfast, and how Mr Fairbairn was expecting a telephone call from the Prime Minister. When the call came, the butler made sure he was in the best position to overhear something about the cause of all this perturbation.

The master of the house listened frowningly as the Prime Minister explained.

As far as Scoggins could make out, there were important visitors they must do their best to entertain. This very evening. A splendid diplomatic dinner must be arranged – at once.

The call ended abruptly and Mr Fairbairn started issuing instructions immediately to the butler, who blanched at the extra work involved. 'I know it is very short notice,' his master told him, 'But I have every faith that Cook and your staff can pull off a state banquet in the allotted time. That is why the Prime Minister has chosen us for this honour.'

Scoggins was flattered by these words. As they walked to the front hall Mr Fairbairn added, 'These are extremely important visitors, Scoggins. They have come an immensely long distance. It is vital to the country that the evening's entertainment goes well. All the cabinet will be here. All the great and the good of our nation.'

Scoggins watched his master hasten out of the house to his car, which was waiting to take him to the House of Commons.

Then the butler marched stiffly downstairs into the servants' hall, where he was the bearer of exciting tidings. Cook went ballistic, of course. She went up like a barrage balloon in a flurry of temperament and agitation, sending kitchen maids scuttling into action.

In all the confusion, Scoggins stopped to consider what kind of delegation this might be. Who was important enough that the whole British government had to be assembled to receive them, and at such short notice? Where had these foreigners come from?

Meanwhile the Doctor was examining the empty office of the dooryard. The place looked as if it had been abandoned in a rush.

As he mooched around the place he heard a squeaking of castors close by.

'Hello?'

There came another nervous squeak, just behind him.

'Who's there?' urged the Doctor.

The shabby green door trailing him gave a little cough. And then, to the Doctor's complete astonishment, it spoke. 'Knock knock!' the Door said nervously.

The Doctor cried out: 'WHAT?!'

'I was never very good at sneaking about,' the Door explained glumly. 'And of course, my 'knock knock' is hopeless. I just tend to shout the words.'

The Doctor had communicated with some strange creatures in his time, but never a Door. 'Crikey! Look at you! Hello, I'm the Doctor. And you're a Door! A talking Door! So... what's the story? Are you all alive then?'

'Most of us are hibernating.' The Door's voice seemed to be issuing from his silver knocker, shaped like a lion's head. 'It's been a long journey. And I've personally been working very hard to master your human languages so I can act as the intermediary between humankind and we Doors.'

'Blimey!' said the Doctor. 'You've learned every human language? Where did you get your dictionaries? A door-to-door salesman?'

The Door was perplexed. 'I spent some time away from my people, in order to plug my consciousness into one of the finest artificial linguistic intelligences in our galaxy.'

'And – bingo! All human languages are at your fingertips. Uh, well, your, um, letterbox. Never mind. I'm glad you can talk. So am I the first person you've talked to, then?'

The door said, 'No, the first person I spoke to was someone they call the Prime Minister of England.'

The Doctor whistled. 'You don't mess about, do you?'

'I'm making contact in the correct way, according to all the rules of polite etiquette between planets. We're meeting the government, you know. Having dinner with them tonight, I believe.'

The Doctor raised an eyebrow at this. Then he was amazed to learn that the Door didn't have a name. 'What about John Henry?' the Doctor suggested. 'We'll call you after the man who invented the doorbell.'

The Door looked blank. 'What's a doorbell?'

'What's a doorbell?' The Doctor was incredulous. 'You mean, you don't know what a doorbell is?! But... but that's just what you need! You, with your too-quiet knock-knock! Why don't I dig one out of my supplies? I'm sure I've got one. As a kind of welcome to Earth, eh? What do you say? It's bound to impress all the

other Doors. You'll be going 'Ding dong!' then. You could even have a customised tune.'

'Could I?' gasped John Henry.

'It'll be no bother,' grinned the Doctor. He suspected the Door was up to something, of course. Though he thought John Henry might like to be the proud owner of a doorbell anyway. What Door wouldn't?

Mary should have been immersed in preparations for the grand dinner, but she couldn't push out of her mind the terrible things that had happened at the dooryard last night.

She crept along the alleyway and was just in time to see the gate being shunted open by that same skinny man with the strange hair. She gasped then, as a whole phalanx of brightly-painted Doors came issuing out. They squeaked into the quiet lane and stood in stiff formation, paintwork gleaming.

That man was talking with one of them. Talking to the Doors! Mary felt her senses reeling. She went as close as she could. With

an awful sick feeling she realised that one of the Doors was actually talking back. But it couldn't be, could it? Not really. Mary started praying silently.

'Shame the others can't talk,' mused the Doctor. 'I'd like to hear what they've got to say for themselves.' He gave John Henry's newly-fitted bell a firm *trr–iii–nng*.

The Door shivered with noisy pleasure. 'Doors, on the whole, are not very patient at learning new languages, Doctor. Only I was prepared to take the time to go and study.'

'They don't like to hang around,' the Doctor nodded. It was a bit creepy, he thought, the way the other Doors – about thirty of them – were just faintly rattling their door furniture.

John Henry told the Doctor what they were saying. It was basically this: they wanted help in their dealings with the human beings. 'We want nothing but lasting peace between us and them. Will you open doors for us with the British government?'

The Doctor was just about to say that he would be delighted when there came an awful squeal from the shadows. He spun round on one heel. 'What?!'

There was a girl there. A very pretty girl in a maid's drab uniform. She was emerging from hiding, her face etched with horror.

'You can't go working with them! My fella – he was spirited away by them!'

The Doctor caught hold of the girl. He was aware of the army of Doors staring at them both. 'You're the girl I saw last night! What was wrong with you, eh? You ran off before I could ask. Calm down and tell me now.'

Gabbling breathlessly, Mary told the awful story of how she and her young man had been menaced by these weird living Doors in the dead of night.

'Erm,' said the Doctor. 'I dunno how they'll feel about being called weird living doors. They seem okay to me. Pretty approachable, really.'

'Tell that to Tommy!' cried Mary. 'They took him, those things! Took him away from me!'

John Henry squeaked closer. He whispered, 'Whatever does the girl mean?'

Mary shrieked at the Door's approach. 'Keep it away from me! How can it talk? It's a Door! It's a talking Door!'

The Doctor patted her shoulder awkwardly. 'What you've got to understand, is that there are all kinds of living, reasoning beings in the universe, Mary. They come in multifarious shapes and sizes. I've seen things you would never believe. And now I've seen Doors that can talk. And so have you. Say hello to John Henry, Mary.'

Mary tutted at him. 'I've seen Doors before. But I've never had the heebie-jeebies off of 'em.'

'Doctor?' John Henry interrupted. 'The others are agitated. They feel that this girl might dissuade you from our cause. And they want to know... will you still go with us tonight? To meet the leaders of this country? At the reception dinner at somewhere called 256 Beaton Square?'

Mary broke away, squawking loudly. 'But that's my place! That's the house where I work! How does that Door know where I live?'

'Hmmm,' mused the Doctor. 'Why not? Of course I'll be there. I wouldn't miss this for the world.'

Everyone agreed that Cook outdid herself with that diplomatic banquet. Whipping up salmon mousses. Roasting half a lamb. Creating a dessert like you wouldn't believe. The servants slaved over the sparkling crystal and silver. All of them wondering what exotic kind of foreigners they were going to be serving that evening.

Mary just got on with her work, tight-lipped. She'd promised that strange Doctor no trouble, and he had a certain... way about him. Mary thought she could trust him.

Excitement grew as the guests gathered. All were resplendent in evening dress. The women in gorgeous frocks. The servants on the stairs, watching.

At the appointed hour a van pulled up outside of the house. Scoggins the butler scathingly observed that it looked rather like a furniture van.

Then – out came a whole set of doors. Gleaming, buffed up. Door furniture shining. These foreigners were impressively smart, but they were Doors.

Of course, all of the guests at the house in Beaton Square were far too well-bred and polite to draw attention to this fact.

The only human figure accompanying the Doors was a lanky man in evening dress, seemingly their friend. As he introduced the British cabinet to the alien Doors he gave Mary a broad wink that Scoggins didn't miss.

Then came the moment for John Henry – the Door that had learned to speak English – to address the master of the house.

Some of the ladies had to sit down, feeling faint at this point.

'We have journeyed through the inchoate wilderness of outer space,' John Henry said. 'We are here to bring you our wisdom from the stars.'

Polite applause at this. Then Scoggins bonged the gong and everyone proceeded into the dining room.

The Doors were shown to their places at the table – some chairs having hastily been removed – and dinner commenced. The Doctor tucked in happily. He noticed that John Henry flapped his letter box a couple of times, mimicking the eating motions made by the humans. The other Doors stood impassively by their untouched plates and John Henry skilfully interpreted their various knockings and bangings. They had many flattering things to say about this city they were visiting.

Mary hovered about the table with the crystal decanters.

As the meal went on the humans grew excited at the idea of life from beyond. 'Where is your space vessel?' the Prime Minister's wife burst out. The Doctor noted the greedy glint in the Prime Minister's eye. He knew the old man was wondering, 'What can we get out of you lot, eh? How can we exploit this remarkable turn of events?'

The Doctor watched one of the junior ministers slipping out of the dining room. Then, one of the Doors slid out after him. Presumably the Doors didn't need to go to the lav?

The Doctor hastened out. He followed the squeaks of the Door as it pursued the junior minister into the dark recesses of the house.

Aha, thought the Doctor. The minister was on the phone. Whispering urgently. Blabbing away. Who to? The papers maybe. But there he was. Sweating and scared. Telling someone all about these strange visitors from space. The Doctor sighed. There was always one who tried to spoil it for everyone else.

But before the Doctor could intercede, the Door between them squeaked stealthily across the parquet floor. It stood behind the minister, who went quiet as that oblong shadow fell across him.

He dropped the phone and whirled round. 'Oh God! Oh no!'

The Door clicked ominously. Its hinges squealed. It crept open with horrible slowness.

'No!' yelled the Doctor. But it was too late.

In one terrible moment the Door swallowed up the junior minister, the telephone, and the console table, all in one go. WHOMP. It slammed shut abruptly and there was silence.

Then the Door swung round to face the Doctor…

Without any further ado, the Doctor hurtled back to the dining room. The ladies had gracefully retired and it was time for brandy and cigars. The Doctor stormed straight over to John Henry and glowered at the friendly Door. 'What are you lot playing at? I believed in you! You said you'd come here in peace! But what do I find? WHOMP. That's what. You're just another load of alien invaders!'

John Henry stared at him. 'What? But I told the truth!'

'Look,' the Doctor began. 'I've just seen–'

But John Henry interrupted him. 'Not now, Doctor. I've got important diplomatic work to attend to.' Then the green Door bustled over to the fireplace, where the high commanders of the Doors were standing with the Prime Minister. He shut me up! The Doctor thought furiously. I've been shut up… by a Door!

'My leaders are very pleased that you have welcomed us with open arms, sir,' John Henry was translating for the benefit of the premier and his various ministers. 'And, erm, we Doors are here to usher in a new way of life… and a new regime…'

The Prime Minister stroked his mutton chop whiskers. 'Hang on a sec, old man, I'm not sure I follow…'

The Doctor burst in rudely, shouting out: 'Oh, I follow all right! I know what they're up to! They're not so peaceful as they seem! They're here to invade you!'

The clustered politicians chuckled at this. 'What can a bunch of Doors do to us? They're just Doors!'

As they laughed heartily, one of the main Doors suddenly flew open. The Doctor didn't have time to act.

WHOMP. The Door swallowed up the Prime Minister. He was gone. Just a little curl of cigar smoke was all that remained.

There was a stunned silence, and then the cabinet ministers started shrieking. In the hubbub, John Henry carried on interpreting, worriedly.

'We met your leaders here for a purpose tonight. You will all be... dispatched!' The translator Door looked very upset by now. 'Oh, Doctor! What have I done? I've been a fool!'

The Doors were so pleased with themselves that they didn't notice John Henry flying off the handle. He turned on a castor and stormed out of the room. He pushed past Scoggins, the appalled butler, and headed for the exit. He wanted nothing to do with an invasion.

After a few minutes the alien beings realised that their translator had gone. Their leader was outraged. They were all knocking like mad as they hurried after him.

The Doctor gave chase. In the hallway he was met by Mary. 'The Prime Minister..?'

'WHOMPED!' shouted the Doctor, and grabbed her hand, pulling her after him. They slipped past the confused, awkward Doors lumbering down the hall.

Out in the street they found the furniture van, and the disconsolate John Henry, who didn't know where to go.

'Honestly, Doctor. I didn't know their plans. I really thought we were here to make friends. Not this!'

The Doctor patted him. 'I believe you. Mary, help John Henry. We're stealing this van. We're taking him to the TARDIS.'

Mary did as she was told, wondering what a TARDIS was.

'That'll spoil their plans, being without their translator,' said the Doctor. He cast a glance back to the big house. 'Come on! They'll be after us!'

Sure enough, the other Doors were coming through the porch, banging into pillars and posts in their haste, and bouncing down the front steps.

'Giddyap!' cried the Doctor and the horses responded. The furniture van leapt into action, knocking Mary and John Henry off balance.

With a manic grin, the Doctor took the reins and urged the horses out of the sedate London square. The horses snorted in alarm but soon plunged into action. Their hooves rang loudly on the road as they pulled the carriage through several quiet streets and squares.

As they turned the corner onto a rather busier route, a London Bobby blew his whistle hard at them. The Doctor urged them on faster, caroming madly round several corners sharply, narrowly missing a pillar box and an old flower seller who was sent sprawling with her wares across the pavement.

'Whoops! Sorry!' yelled the Doctor, back over his shoulder. But now he was getting used to keeping the carriage on the straight and narrow. The van tore off in the direction of the Thames.

Back at Beaton Square, the Doors had watched them go. They rattled and knocked with fury. They were missing their translator already. They couldn't command the humans to do anything!

The humans – still in a state of shock – watched the party of six Doors assembling in the street.

'Saints preserve us,' whispered the butler Scoggins, as the Doors lifted into the air. 'They can fly!'

The Doors slid smoothly into the clear air, sailing like heavy surfboards into the sky. In tight formation they swept grandly over the heads of the terrified ministers and servants and streaked off after the Doctor and the van.

The Doors soared over high rooftops and panned out: scanning the cobbled streets and main roads for the fleeing furniture van.

And then they found their quarry. Tearing full tilt along the Embankment.

'I mean it,' said John Henry as the Doctor spurred the horses on. 'I really didn't know that they were planning on attacking human beings or invading. They kept all those plans from me. They probably decided it all while I was away, on my language course...'

'All right! All right, I believe you!' The Doctor really did believe him, but didn't want to hear all of John Henry's thoughts about the matter while they were in the middle of running away. Another shrill whistle filled the air, and he realized that another policeman had caught them speeding.

Just then, Mary shrieked: 'Doctor!' She was pointing at the sky behind them. She could hardly believe what she was seeing. 'Oh, my word!'

'What is it?' yelled the Doctor. He couldn't take his eyes off the road, as, on this busier section, the traffic was going mad all around them. Snorting horses and steaming motor cars. Honking and screeching as they whipped from one side of the road to the other. He kept the horses ducking and weaving away from collisions but it was just a matter of time before something went dreadfully wrong...

'DOORS!!' Mary screamed in his ear, and he whipped his head around to see.

'Oh no. That's no good. They can fly!' He shouted at John Henry. 'You can FLY?!'

Shame-facedly, John Henry admitted that most of his kind could.

'Brilliant,' groaned the Doctor. 'Well, that makes it nearly impossible for us to get away from them in a furniture van.'

'How can Doors fly?!' Mary shrieked, clinging on for dear life. With every passing second those deadly-looking Doors were swooping closer.

'Because they're not just Doors as you understand Doors,' gabbled the Doctor. 'You see, they're each little rips in time and space. Living apertures into some nightmarish universe, given sentience and... and little wheels!'

Mary was not at all sure what he was saying.

'Doctor, look out!' cried John Henry over his shoulder. His doorbell trilled fiercely as the Doctor narrowly avoided a fruit cart.

The Doctor was still talking. 'They obviously took the form of Doors as something very familiar to humankind. Something we use everyday. Whose idea was that?'

'Mine,' said John Henry. 'I really had no idea that they meant to do such awful things. Like I say, I was busy studying...'

'They want to destabilise Earth by swallowing up its leaders, and then gradually getting rid of all living beings. Presumably, leaving a world of all doors and no people.'

Mary's mind was boggling at this.

It was just at the moment they thought they had miraculously broken free and lost their pursuers that they were caught. The van was hurtling along beside the glittering Thames when Mary cried out.

There, in the pale skies ahead of them, the Doors were tumbling through the clear air. They had soared ahead and were spinning towards the horses at speed.

WHOMP. The Doors flew open at just the right moment and swallowed the horses one after the next. Mary screamed as the carriage swerved madly sideways.

WHOMP. WHOMP. The Doors came flapping after them with deadly precision.

Even with the horses gone, the van carried on bounding along for quite some way. The shafts screeched, smouldered and sparked; the wheels buckled and flew apart. In a matter of seconds the wooden framework was shaken into smithereens. The wreckage slewed sideways and came to a resounding splintery standstill at the side of the road.

The Doctor and his friends were flung to the ground. The Doctor banged his head on John Henry's doorbell. DRR-iii-nnnggg!

They sat up groggily, full of scrapes and bruises, but mostly, amazingly, unhurt. The Doctor was helped to his feet by Mary.

He looked around and saw, with a sinking feeling in both his hearts, that they were surrounded by Doors.

They were hemmed in on all sides and there was surely no way out for them now.

The Doctor started shouting, rapidly and with great authority, brandishing his sonic. 'Okay! If you back off right now and stop all of this, I'll forget it ever happened. Do you hear me? I'm giving you a chance, all right? If you return the Prime Minister and the poor horses and all the others…'

'And my Tommy!' shouted Mary, shaking her small fist.

There was some knocking, and John Henry translated. 'They say that all of those organisms have been sent to the noxious world from which we Doors originate. That's why we want a new world. Our old one is poisonous and stinky.'

'Bring them back,' said the Doctor menacingly.

'They won't listen, Doctor,' John Henry said. 'They want the whole world. And I helped them!'

Mary patted the green Door. 'You weren't to know. Was he, Doctor?'

Just then the Doctor was more concerned by the fact that the invaders were boxing them in. He knew that in only a few seconds the Doors would open and WHOMP them into another world. He had to start thinking fast.

'Waitwaitwait! Talk to me, Doors! We can work this out!'

But the Doors were pressing from all sides. They were getting closer and forming a cube about their prey. A deadly wooden cube.

'They say there is no escape,' said John Henry, as Mary clung to him and it grew darker. 'There's NO EXIT!!'

'I'm so sorry I have to resort to this,' said the Doctor sadly. He reached out and rang John Henry's doorbell. *TRRrrrr–iiii–IINNGGGGGGG!*

Mary was disappointed. 'What's that meant to do?'

The Doctor held his sonic up to the doorbell button. 'Cover your ears.'

Almost instantly they were engulfed by huge distorting waves of sound. It was like being inside the towers of Notre Dame. The soundwaves billowed and rippled crazily.

Mary screamed, trying to shut out the noise of the infinitely deadly ding-dong. It was the worst noise she had ever heard.

The effect on the attacking Doors was even more remarkable.

After a while the Doctor stopped ringing the bell and disconnected the sonic.

The Doors were simply standing there.

'Have you killed them?' Mary asked, her head ringing with after-echoes.

'I've deafened them,' said the Doctor.

John Henry listened for the knocking of his nefarious masters. Nothing.

The Doctor said, 'They can't articulate or communicate. They can't do anything.' But then he looked sadly at John Henry. 'But I'm afraid the same goes for John Henry here. He's cut off from everyone, too, without his hearing.'

Mary looked at the stilled, silent doors.

'Brilliant, eh?' grinned the Doctor. 'I've trounced them! With no communication between them, there's no coordination. I've ruined their invasion plans!'

As if to prove his success, the Doctor went up to the leader.

Knock knock. The Door simply fell down with a resounding crash. A few seconds later, the others followed, like a series of tall dominoes. He opened one up. There was nothing beyond. 'No alien dimension,' said the Doctor, almost regretfully. 'Nothing. Just Doors that aren't going anywhere.'

Mary tried to smile. She tried to be pleased. But she was too busy thinking about John Henry.

Just in case it all went wrong, the Doctor left Mary at home when he went spinning off in the TARDIS to find the world that the Doors had come from. All the information he needed was back at the dooryard, which turned out to be the Doors' weirdly wooden spaceship in disguise.

It was the simple work of a morning, journeying to that faraway planet and returning the would-be wooden invaders. While he was there, the Doctor picked up various bewildered victims: junior ministers, the Prime Minister, those coach horses and, of course, Mary's young man, Tommy.

The Doctor still felt quite sad about John Henry. Without him, thwarting the Doors would have been so much harder.

When he returned to 256 Beaton Square he found Mary hard at work. She was round the back, replacing the old door. She'd

hated that old door with Scoggins' spyhole. When the Doctor arrived she was in the last stages of fitting John Henry into place in the threshold.

'Tommy!' Mary screamed, as she turned to see her young man standing there with the Doctor. 'Where've you been?'

'Uh…' said Tommy.

'John Henry!' cried the Doctor, hurrying over, to where the green Door stood very proudly and smartly at the entrance to the servants' quarters. 'He looks almost pleased to be there,' the Doctor told Mary.

The Doctor reached out and rang the doorbell.

Trr–iii–nng John Henry went. And who was to say it wasn't a contented sound?

Unfortunately it brought Scoggins the butler running.

'What are you lot doing, hanging around here? Who's that boy you're with, Mary? And who's this man? And what have you done with the old door? And my spyhole?'

Mary hissed to the Doctor. 'He doesn't remember anything about the foiled invasion and the Doors. None of them do! Not even the Prime Minister!'

The Doctor nodded, giving John Henry a farewell pat. 'The vibrations of the doorbell, ringing through the dimensions, were enough to wipe almost everyone's memory of the few days' bizarre events. Thank goodness.'

'Haven't you heard me?' grimaced the butler. 'We don't like strangers round here, banging on our back doors!'

'Bye, Mary,' smiled the Doctor. 'Tommy, you take good care of her. And look after John Henry, will you? Give him a bit of a polish now and then?'

'Are you sure you won't step inside for a bit, Doctor?' Mary asked. 'Have a cup of tea and a bit of cake?'

But the stranger had already hurried off down the lane. He turned and gave a cheery wave.

Trrrr–iiiiii–nnnngggg…! went the doorbell, of its own accord.

THE END

The Haldenmor Fugue

WRITTEN BY **JAMES MORAN** ILLUSTRATIONS BY **ANDY WALKER**

'The trouble with travelling on your own for so long,' said the Doctor, 'is that you end up talking to yourself a lot. Like now, I suppose.'

The TARDIS lurched to one side alarmingly, and the Doctor held on to a lever to stop himself from falling. He raced around the central console, flicking switches, pulling levers, and hammering bits of it, until the lurching settled down. He slumped down in his chair and wiped his forehead, exhausted.

'You also have to do all of the work yourself. Blimey. Still, keeps me fit I suppose. All right, look, this is ridiculous – stop talking to yourself, right now. Right now!'

He stopped talking, but then couldn't bear the silence.

'I suppose thinking out loud isn't the same as talking to yourself, is it? No, of course not. As long as you don't answer. Which I just did, but that doesn't count.'

He stared at the scanner screen, frowning.

'Now, that shouldn't be there. Why's that there? Eh? I'll tell you why that's there. It's there... because something's gone wrong. Temporal fluctuations, spatial drift, and – something else.'

He tapped at the keyboard, tightening the focus of the scan. He frowned again.

'No, that's all wrong, there's a whole set of timelines going off in completely the wrong direction. Somebody's messing about with time and causing trouble. And that's *my* job...'

He yanked a lever, and ran over to the door. He looked back for a moment. He had got used to introducing people to new planets, new times, new aliens. Now it was just him, the universe felt just a tiny bit less exciting.

'When you're showing someone around your home town, it always seems more fun,' he murmured to himself. He shook it off, and fixed a big smile to his face. 'Never mind that, let's have a look at you.'

He flung open the doors and stepped outside, where a large, ultra modern Earth city awaited him. Skyscrapers gleamed in the sunshine, and birds sang in the small park the TARDIS had landed in.

'Earth! Ah, still smells the same – mud, salt water, and chips, no matter where you land. Funny that. Anyway, Earth! The year 2180, eastern England, the great city of...' He tailed off. 'Actually, I haven't got a clue. Excuse me!'

He stopped an elderly man walking his dog. 'What city is this?'

The dog walker looked at him. 'Haldenmor, of course. What else would it be?'

'I don't know, that's why I asked. Could be anywhere, couldn't it? Well, not the shipyards of Tregenna IV, it couldn't be those, they got pulled into a mini-black hole. No, you're right, now you mention it, there's an awful lot of places it couldn't be. Sorry, I'm babbling, I've been on my own for a while.'

The old man leaned in close, sniffing.

'Are you drunk? Eh? At this time of the day?'

'No, I just didn't know where I'd landed.'

The old man shook his head, not convinced.

'Hmph. Youngsters.'

'Actually, I'm older than you,' said the Doctor. 'I know, I don't look it. Want to know my secret? Run everywhere, and drink lots of water.'

The old man wandered off, muttering to himself. The Doctor smiled. 'Now, where to?'

As if on cue, there were several loud screams from a nearby building. The Doctor grinned, and started running. 'They're playing my song,' he announced to nobody in particular. Then frowned yet again. 'I really must stop talking to myself.'

The Doctor ran into the reception area of the skyscraper, a task made more difficult by the crowd of terrified people streaming out of it. Finally he made it through, and strode forward to the reception desk, which was abandoned.

'Hello?' he called. 'Shop?'

No answer. Just then, a female security guard came walking around the corner, shouting into her walkie-talkie. She was in her mid-thirties, serious, and looked like she could beat up dinosaurs with one of her eyebrows.

'Ground floor clear, let me know as soon as you've checked out the loading zone, then we can start getting everyone back in. Can I help you?'

The Doctor realised she meant him. 'Oh! Sorry, thought you were – blimey, still using walkie-talkies in 2180? Mind you, I suppose they're reliable, can't really argue with the technology. Well, you can, but it doesn't argue back, unless it's become self-aware or something, and then you're in trouble. I'm the Doctor, by the way. Hello! What's your name?'

'Carla. Could you wait outside please?'

'Nice to meet you, Carla.'

The Doctor stuck his hand out, and Carla found herself shaking it without quite knowing why. The Doctor waved the psychic paper at her.

'And I'd love to wait outside, but unfortunately for me, I'm the building inspector. Having some sort of trouble?'

Carla sighed. 'You could say that. All the fire alarms went off on the third floor, and everyone swears they saw ghosts coming through the walls. Which part of the Building Inspection Handbook would that come under, do you think?'

The Doctor thought for a moment. 'That would be Chapter 28: Weird Stuff.' He grinned, a grin so wide and dazzling, you couldn't help but be charmed by it. Unless you were Carla, who really wasn't in the mood today. She stared at him.

'You'll be wanting to come and have a look, then?'

The Doctor's grin faltered and disappeared. 'Yeah, may as well, while I'm here. You enjoy your job, Carla?'

'Yes. Except days like this.'

They walked over to the lifts together.

'Oh, I don't know,' said the Doctor. 'Makes it more interesting, I think.'

'There you go, then.'

They entered the lift in silence. As the lift brought them up, the Doctor tried again.

'So what do they do here, in this building?'

'It's an accountancy firm. They do accounts.'

'Right. So no research laboratories, physics experimentation, anything like that?'

'No. They do accounts.'

'Gotcha. Who do they do accounts for, anyone interesting, or famous?'

'I don't know. They don't let me go nosing through their confidential client lists, for some reason.'

Silence again. The lift crawled towards the third floor.

'Not much for small talk, are you, Carla?' said the Doctor.

'Not particularly. Whereas you seem unable to cope unless someone is talking. Usually you.'

'True. But I am very interesting, you have to admit.'

Carla glared at him, but said nothing.

'Maybe not, then,' said the Doctor.

Ding! The doors opened on to a large open-plan office. The Doctor and Carla walked in, looking around.

'Must have been a false alarm,' said Carla. 'I've shut down the fire alarms for this floor, we'll get them checked out.'

'What about the reports that people saw ghosts?'

'I'll check the ghost detectors too. If any ghosts did come through here, they should have picked up something.'

The Doctor nodded, then realised what Carla had said. 'You don't have ghost detectors, do you?'

'No. I was being sarcastic. People were panicking, they imagined things. There's no such thing as ghosts.'

'True. But there are lots of other things in this universe, some of which might look like ghosts. Too early to tell, though.'

'Have you seen enough? I need to start getting everyone back in.'

The Doctor opened his mouth to speak, but just before he could say anything, the lights flickered in the room. One section of wall shimmered, and suddenly changed. Instead of a flat, white office wall, it was now a lumpy, earthen wall, with a flaming torch fastened to it. Part of the carpeting was now a dirty floor covered in sawdust. The two different environments were somehow merged together, overlapping.

'Oh, now that's interesting,' said the Doctor. A spark from the flaming torch rose up, floated towards them, and landed on a sheet of paper on a nearby desk. The sheet of paper started burning where the spark had landed. The Doctor blew the flame out, and showed the burnt paper to Carla.

'Definitely not a ghost,' he said, as Carla touched the scorched paper wonderingly.

Footsteps approached them, heavy, marching footsteps that made the ground shake. But there was nobody else to be seen in the room. Carla's eyes darted around, and she drew her gun.

'Hold your horses there, Carla,' said the Doctor. 'Let's not jump to conclusions. We don't know if it's a threat.'

Then, out of nowhere, a group of about twenty men marched through the office, appearing out of thin air, walking over the strange, sawdust-covered ground. They were carrying spears, round, wooden shields, and wore conical, hard leather helmets. They spotted the Doctor and Carla, and roared in anger. The men started running towards them, lowering their spears to attack.

'Well,' said Carla, managing to maintain her composure with a visible effort, 'how about now? Would you say this is a threat or not?'

She aimed her gun at the approaching men. But just as they reached the edge of the sawdust and stepped forward on to the office carpeting, they vanished, as if they had slipped behind an invisible shield.

The footsteps kept on coming towards the Doctor and Carla, but went right past them, fading away gradually.

The wall containing the flaming torch shimmered again, and disappeared, returning to normal. Now it was just a plain office wall once again.

The Doctor ran over to it, and felt around, double-checking it with his sonic screwdriver.

'This isn't right,' he muttered. 'This isn't right at all. It just shouldn't be here. Why is it here?'

'What's going on?' demanded Carla. 'You're not a building inspector. So who are you?'

'Why'd you say I'm not a building inspector?'

'Because if you were, that would've made you run away screaming.'

'Good point. So why didn't you run away, screaming?'

'Because I'm brave. And I have a gun, they only had spears.'

'Yeah, but there were twenty of them.'

'I'm fast. Who *are* you?'

'I told you. I'm the Doctor. And no, I'm not a building inspector. But I knew something weird was going on here, and now I need to figure out what it is. I can fix this. Trust me.'

Carla stared into the Doctor's face. Then nodded. 'Fair enough. I need to get my building back and stop this from happening again. So I'm coming with you.'

The Doctor hesitated. 'Is there any way I can stop you doing that?'

Carla shook her head, and put away her gun. 'No. But go ahead and try, if it makes you feel better. I'll tell everyone you put up a good fight.'

'No, that's fine, thanks. Come on.'

'Where?'

'Well, I came here when I picked up traces of temporal fluctuation. It's all over this city, and if I narrow the search beam, I can pinpoint the location.'

He took out his sonic, and did a quick scan. 'This building is a bit of a hot spot. But there's another one fairly close by. Let's see what's going on.'

'And what then? You can fix it?'

The Doctor hesitated. 'Yes. And then everything will be back to normal. Come on!'

He hurried off, covering his brief moment of hesitation. But Carla had spotted it, and was worried. Something about this felt wrong to her. She trusted this mad stranger for some reason, but knew that he wasn't telling her everything. For now though, she'd just have to wait and see what happened.

The Doctor and Carla ran down the street, following the signal, which led them straight into a busy shopping centre.

'What are we looking for?' asked Carla.

'Anything out of the ordinary,' said the Doctor. 'Like that!' He pointed. A patch of sawdust had appeared on the ground, and was growing.

'It's happening again. It's changing the ground and anything it touches. Keep back!'

Suddenly the patch of new ground tripled in size, and enveloped one of the shops, completely transforming it into a large mud shack, with smoke coming out of a hole in the roof. Shoppers fled the shack in panic, some still holding the clothes they had picked out from racks that were no longer there.

And then they heard the marching sound again. The Doctor waved his hands around at the shoppers, shouting at them.

'Run! Get out of here! Go!'

Most of them ignored him. Until the group of twenty armed warriors appeared. The warriors drew closer together, forming a fighting unit, and charged a group of shoppers. The Doctor ran over to help, and Carla was right there beside him. She went for her gun, but he stopped her.

'No! That's not how we do things. They're not our enemy, they're just confused and scared. They think we're the enemy. Don't hurt them!'

Carla didn't seem too happy about it, but did as he said. They reached the warriors, and started shouting to distract them, trying to lead them away from the terrified shoppers.

'Hey! Hey! Over here! Come on, attack us instead, we'll be more fun!' yelled the Doctor.

'Get away from them!' shouted Carla. 'Come on! Come on, we'll take you all on!'

'That's the spirit,' said the Doctor. 'Always expect to win.'

'Oh, I *would* win,' said Carla.

The warriors turned to face them.

'Right,' said the Doctor. 'Looks like

you'll get to test that theory. Still, at least they're chasing us and not innocent shoppers.'

'Stop talking, and run!'

The Doctor and Carla ran further into the now empty shopping centre, and the warriors kept coming.

'We need to get past them without getting stuck with the sharp end of those spears,' said the Doctor. 'Look for something we can defend ourselves with.'

'I do have a perfectly good gun,' said Carla.

'No, I told you, that's not how we do it.'

'How about those then?'

She pointed at the nearest shop.

The Doctor grinned. 'Perfect!'

They disappeared inside the shop. The warriors approached steadily, lowering their shields to take a closer look. The leader stared at the shop window, which said *Sports Equipment: SALE!*

Then, with a war cry, the Doctor and Carla came running out of the shop. They were covered in cricketing gear – shin pads, thigh pads, arm guards, chest pads, helmets with titanium grilles, gloves – and they were wielding cricket bats.

'Right,' shouted the Doctor. 'We'll bat first!'

He looked at Carla, nodded, and they charged straight for the warriors, keeping their heads down. The first few warriors tried to spear them, but were swiftly deflected with the bats and protective gear. 'Howzat!' said the Doctor, enjoying himself. Carla slammed more warriors aside, knocking them over with great enthusiasm. One adventurous warrior drew a sword, and tried to fight it out. The Doctor raised his cricket bat, only to have it sliced in half by a sword.

'Oi!' he said. 'That's not cricket!'

He ducked as the sword came back for another go, then managed to trip the warrior up and keep going. Carla faced down a warrior who was taking great swipes at her with a two-handed axe. The axe was so big, it slowed him down considerably – so Carla waited until he was on the downswing, and then kicked him, hard, sending him flying through the window of a sweet shop. A huge tray of pick and mix sweets came pouring out of the broken window. Several warriors skidded around on the sweets, losing their balance. The Doctor plucked a jelly baby from the air before it could touch the floor, popped it in his mouth, and brandished his broken cricket bat, ready to take on the next warrior.

But then, with a shimmer, they all vanished, and the shopping centre was back to normal. Apart from the mess of broken glass and ruined shop windows.

'Right,' said the Doctor, getting his breath back. 'Nice bit of defensive work there. I think we can safely claim victory.'

'So who are they?' asked Carla. 'They're not ghosts. They're from the past, aren't they?'

'Yep. And I think I know what's going on. Where's the nearest library?'

The Doctor and Carla marched into the library, still dressed in their protective cricket gear. The Doctor waved cheerfully at the librarian, and headed for the history section.

'Now then, Haldenmor, let's have a look at you. Local history, there we go.'

He pulled a large book down from the shelf, called 'History of Haldenmor'. He flipped through the pages, reading quickly. And stopped smiling.

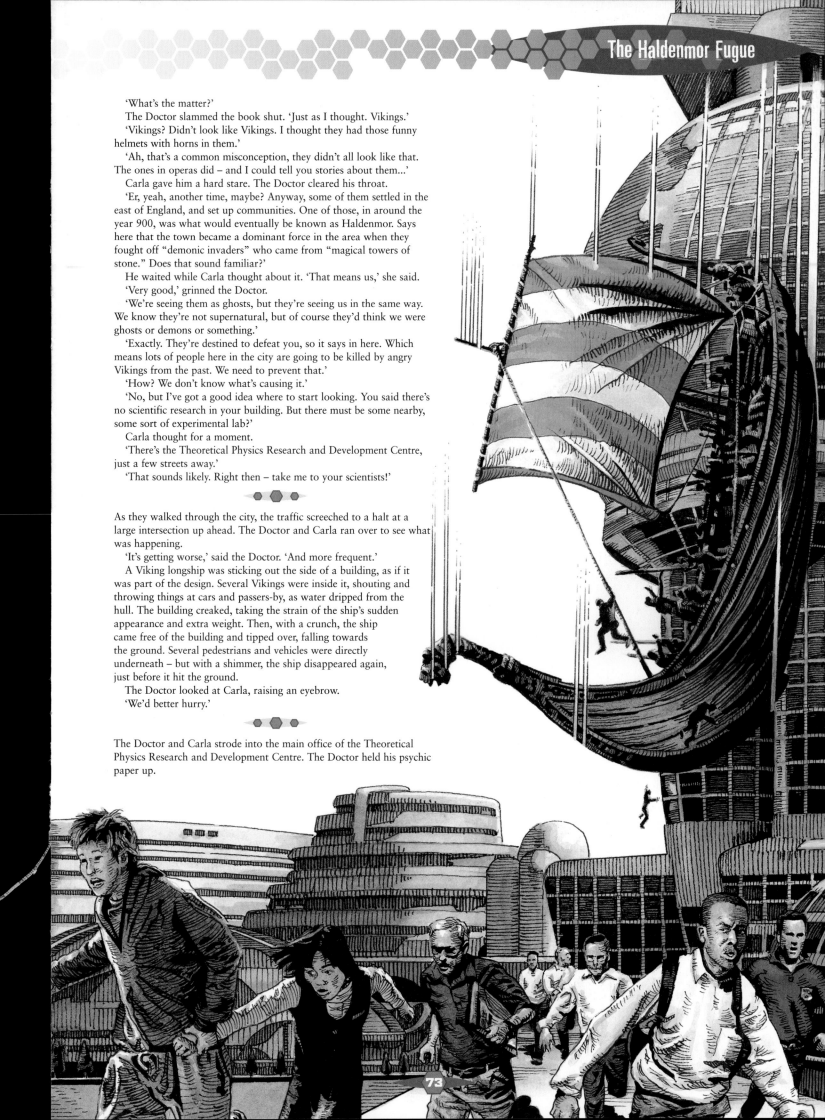

'What's the matter?'

The Doctor slammed the book shut. 'Just as I thought. Vikings.'

'Vikings? Didn't look like Vikings. I thought they had those funny helmets with horns in them.'

'Ah, that's a common misconception, they didn't all look like that. The ones in operas did – and I could tell you stories about them...'

Carla gave him a hard stare. The Doctor cleared his throat.

'Er, yeah, another time, maybe? Anyway, some of them settled in the east of England, and set up communities. One of those, in around the year 900, was what would eventually be known as Haldenmor. Says here that the town became a dominant force in the area when they fought off "demonic invaders" who came from "magical towers of stone." Does that sound familiar?'

He waited while Carla thought about it. 'That means us,' she said.

'Very good,' grinned the Doctor.

'We're seeing them as ghosts, but they're seeing us in the same way. We know they're not supernatural, but of course they'd think we were ghosts or demons or something.'

'Exactly. They're destined to defeat you, so it says in here. Which means lots of people here in the city are going to be killed by angry Vikings from the past. We need to prevent that.'

'How? We don't know what's causing it.'

'No, but I've got a good idea where to start looking. You said there's no scientific research in your building. But there must be some nearby, some sort of experimental lab?'

Carla thought for a moment.

'There's the Theoretical Physics Research and Development Centre, just a few streets away.'

'That sounds likely. Right then – take me to your scientists!'

As they walked through the city, the traffic screeched to a halt at a large intersection up ahead. The Doctor and Carla ran over to see what was happening.

'It's getting worse,' said the Doctor. 'And more frequent.'

A Viking longship was sticking out the side of a building, as if it was part of the design. Several Vikings were inside it, shouting and throwing things at cars and passers-by, as water dripped from the hull. The building creaked, taking the strain of the ship's sudden appearance and extra weight. Then, with a crunch, the ship came free of the building and tipped over, falling towards the ground. Several pedestrians and vehicles were directly underneath – but with a shimmer, the ship disappeared again, just before it hit the ground.

The Doctor looked at Carla, raising an eyebrow.

'We'd better hurry.'

The Doctor and Carla strode into the main office of the Theoretical Physics Research and Development Centre. The Doctor held his psychic paper up.

'Now then! John Smith, Scientific Research Ombudsman, emergency surprise inspection... thingy. Who's in charge here?'

As the staff bustled around to find the boss, Carla whispered to the Doctor. 'When you showed that to me, it said you were a building inspector. How did you manage that?'

'Tricks of the trade, my dear Carla.'

'And what is your trade, exactly?'

'Ooh, bit of this, bit of that. Hello! Are you the big cheese?'

A nervous man in his fifties stood in front of the Doctor, continually trying to stop his glasses from sliding down his nose. 'Er, I suppose, yes, I'm the managing director. Jerry Monroe. I wasn't expecting an inspection.'

'Ah, well, if you were, it wouldn't be a surprise inspection, would it?'

'No, I suppose not. Where did you want to start?'

'Let's start with the research into time travel.'

Monroe stared at the Doctor, shocked. He moved closer, and whispered. 'Nobody – I mean, *nobody* – knows about that.'

'Neither did I, I just assumed. See, there's been quite a large build up of temporal energy and it's caused a teensy bit of a leak in time. That tells me that someone's trying to do something they shouldn't, and they haven't quite got there yet. I'm guessing it's at an early stage.'

'Yes, it's all theoretical, but we have made quite a fascinating breakthrough – sorry, is there some sort of problem with it? It's all just numbers and words right now, it's hardly a danger to anyone.'

The Doctor's face was grim. 'That's where you're wrong. "Just numbers and words"? They're the most dangerous things in the universe. I'll need to take a look.'

In the cramped research office, the Doctor stared at a blackboard filled with a series of equations. He followed the calculations, muttering under his breath.

'Yeah, yeah, gotcha, that bit's slightly clumsy but it gets you there I suppose, right, you've solved that, good, allowed for the coefficient of linear expansion, and – oh, that's very nice...'

He took off his glasses and turned to beam at Monroe. 'You *are* a clever lot! I mean, you won't get there for a while, but you've sussed it, essentially. Thing is, there's a few tiny bits that don't quite fit – nothing terrible, but when you start experimenting on apples and things in, oh, say five years, the temporal fluctuations will be a bit rougher than usual. And it'll cause a rip in space/time. Just a tiny one. But as it goes backwards, it gets bigger and bigger, until you start getting Vikings and longships appearing in the middle of the city.'

'Why does it go backwards?' asked Monroe.

'Doesn't have to. Sometimes it goes forwards. Luck of the draw, really.'

'Well, can't you tell us how to fix it, if it's such a problem?'

'Sorry. Not allowed to. That'd be me giving you secrets you wouldn't have worked out yourself. Someone else will figure it out eventually, just not you.'

'What are you saying?'

'I'm saying, I need to get rid of all your research. This hole in space/time is going to get worse, and the Vikings from the tenth century will come through in force, attack this city, and lots of people will be killed. That's bad enough, but the hole will keep getting bigger, and that'll cause all sorts of bad stuff. I mean, really, *really* bad stuff. You don't even want to know, believe me.'

'Well I'm sorry, but I won't allow it. I'm going to contact the office of the Ombudsman right now, this is outrageous. You can't stop perfectly valid research!'

'You go and call who you like. I'll wait here.'

Monroe stormed out of the office. The Doctor immediately picked up a duster and started wiping the board clean.

'Hey,' said Carla. 'You said you'd wait here.'

'I am waiting here. But I didn't say I wouldn't get started.' He grinned at Carla, and finished wiping the board. He went over to the computer on the desk, and inspected it.

'Right, it's all on here, with a link to the network backup, but I can get to that if I just do this...' He fiddled with the sonic, and the computer beeped, with a message: '*Erase all files and folders: Are you sure? Y/N?*'

The Doctor stopped what he was doing, and turned to Carla. And now, he looked like he had the weight of the universe on his shoulders.

'Oh, Carla, I'm really, truly sorry. But this is goodbye.'

Carla looked away, then spoke quietly. 'It's okay. I figured it out while you were rambling on. You said the town became a dominant force when it defeated the 'demonic invaders', which was us. If you fix the hole, then they never come through and fight us. Which means the town never becomes a dominant force back in the tenth century. Which means it never becomes the city of Haldenmor today. This whole city, as it is right now, ceases to exist.'

The Doctor nodded. 'Pretty much. The city shouldn't be here. Right from the start it just felt wrong, like it was never meant to be.'

'And what about everyone who lives here now?'

'Oh, the people who lived in the town back then would move away, settle somewhere else, so most of the people alive here would still be alive somewhere. Just not here. And they'll have different lives.'

'Most of them? So I'll be born somewhere else? If I'm even born at all?'

'Yep.

'And I won't be a security guard?'

'No idea. You'll have grown up in a different place, with different experiences. Maybe you become a famous opera singer, or a writer, or an explorer. Thing is, I've only known you for a short time, but I can tell that whatever you end up doing, you'll be fantastic.'

'If I'm even born at all.'

'That's right.'

The words hung in the air like toxic smoke. Carla had tears in her eyes, but refused to let them fall.

'This is what you do? You go around fixing things?'

'I try. Doesn't always end well.'

'But you know what's right. I can tell that about you. You know what needs fixing.'

'Yes.'

'Suppose you'd better get on and fix this, then.'

The Doctor nodded. 'It was an absolute pleasure to meet you, Carla. And I wish we could have been friends, because you're so brilliant, and such a laugh – and so serious, *blimey* you're serious, but then that's partly why you're such a laugh. There's so many things I'd love to show you – even just to see the faces you'd pull.'

'And you talk way, way too much.'

The Doctor smiled. 'Guilty.'

'Today was fun,' said Carla. 'I mean, it was weird, and wrong, and silly. But it was really good fun.'

The Doctor felt terrible. This time, there were no monsters to fight, no alien threats to stop, no villains to thwart – just some horribly bad luck that he couldn't do anything about. Carla was wonderful, and it would have been great to bring her along for some adventures. Especially the ones where angry aliens tried to kill him, she'd have been very handy for those. But when he thought about the things that had happened to some of his other travelling companions, maybe she was better off staying here and taking her chances. Even if it meant never being born.

'Well. I'd better finish this.' He pointed at the blinking 'Y/N' on the screen. Carla stood up.

'Promise me something,' she said. 'Promise me, that when it's over, and the city's gone, you'll have a look for me, wherever I end up in the world. If I exist, I mean. See if I was born, if I'm alive. Just... see if I'm okay. And if I don't exist – remember me. Tell stories about me.'

'I promise.'

'Thanks. Now hurry up and fix it, before anything else goes wrong.'

She smiled at him, such a tiny, fragile smile. And for the first time that day – probably the first time in her entire life – she looked scared.

The Doctor hit the 'Y' key, and the files were erased.

And with a shimmer of light, the Doctor was suddenly standing alone in a field, the TARDIS a few hundred yards away. In the ground around him were the faint indentations of an old town.

You'd never notice them if you weren't looking for them. But now, they were all that remained of the tenth-century town that might have become Haldenmor.

Suddenly furious, the Doctor shouted at the sky, at the ground, at nobody in particular.

'Why can't I ever just leave a place the way I found it? Why can't things just turn out all right once in a while? *It's not fair!*'

He sat on the grass, clasping his head in his hands.

Finally, he got up and walked towards the TARDIS. Time to go somewhere else for a while, somewhere far away, somewhere there were no people, no aliens, no problems to solve, nothing. Just peace and quiet, and no heartbreak.

But first, he had a promise to keep.

⬢ ⬢ ⬢

It wasn't easy. There were months of searching through paper records of births and deaths, old family trees filled with inconsistencies, months of dead ends, false alarms, red herrings. In the end, he just went back to tenth century England, and followed every single person from the town through time to see where they ended up – if they got married, had kids, moved, everything. If the family line ended before 2180, he'd go back and start on the next person.

But he'd made a promise, and was determined to see it through.

It took years. *Years.*

Eventually, he found her. Her ancestors had moved from England to Brazil in the late 1600s, which had thrown off his search somewhat. But he tracked her down. She had a different name, of course, in this timeline she was called Yarah, but it was definitely her. It was Carla. This version of Carla was a pilot and, as he had predicted, she was a fantastic one. The Doctor watched her getting ready for a flight, and couldn't stop himself grinning from ear to ear. She was okay. She was alive, and she was happy, and she was brilliant. Still very serious, of course, but some things you're just born with.

'Good on you, Carla,' he whispered.

She caught a glimpse of him as she passed, and wondered why some stranger was grinning at her like an idiot. The Doctor waved, and headed off back to his TARDIS. He'd kept his promise, and could now go and take some time off, away from everyone.

He was so relieved to see her, in fact, that he decided to give her a present, the best present he could possibly think of: he stayed away from her.

But now and again, of course, he dropped in just to make sure she was okay. It was the least he could do for an old friend.

THE END

+++DON'T FORGET ME++++++++++++++

HV8Y78Y23VJHVKY BSWR26R+++ONE LAST LOOK+++GOT TO SEE++++HVF7TR3GROWFK
BEF8Y3MM=F???=WJB3BKJBDHFH - - NDND SPK==

????????????+++CAN'T BE ALIVE! NO! THE GATE+++++Y78Y23VJHV

+++E WATER! GET AWAY FROM THE WAT++++ HJ,VAFHV HBBJSJWWUU73----
73838880YGDD8YGU 9U9U93VIH+++SCANNING, BUT IT MUST++++,JRBGL T999943333

BKSBKGJ-R99332UDN-F-F-FNIII++++NTHEON OF DISCORD, TARGETING HER, NOT HER,
NOT MY WONDERFUL SAR+++++87474VVFBBDBS

+++RISTINA! OUT THERE ON THE MIGHTY 200!+++++KNOCK FOUR TIMES++++KUBK;'ZPFLB
HV8Y78Y23VJHVKY+++I LOVE A BIT OF CHRISTMAS! EVEN WITH THAT CYBER KING.
FUNNY, THAT++++????????????????????????????????

BDBD87883JJSSS+++CURSE, NOT A BLE+++W-S- 'ZPFLBHV8Y78Y23VJHV8OP9L NP'U-
WFDP----I'ZPFLBHV8Y78Y2+++SAYING GOODBYE - SO MANY GOODBY+++

VHJBDGULN DSLIFJF222MMNS KS+++=RIDING THE TARDIS, RIDING THE EARTH, ALL
OF US! THE CHILDREN OF TIME!+++???VB LIBE80 E9933-----2HNFBE DIHS LSMA'"

+++NO, NO DON'T DO THAT, DON'T++++KVHWFVHKFRGUF+++NO SPOILERS!+++

GAIUW8OP9L NP'UWFDP------+++KICKING EDGAR ALLAN+++I---J----PHJKABSFYO
8Y7RT63TRV3WJFVQIYWBBBL KLIAHD;IA;;NNBD2UYERKUBK;'ZPFLBHV8Y78Y23VJHVKY
BSWR26R3EGHVN -- QEIOFJKUBK ALHLK+++IS ENDING SOON+++PROFESSOR SONG?
SONG? SONG! CAMPTOWN RACES???DOODAH, DOODAH+++

+++GATHA CHRISTIE, ONLY TALKING ABOUT YOU THE OTHER D+++HE66EB9D D
IHYUNDNPIDM,Z,Z,+++ON'T EVEN BLINK!+++

IEWGFFIFWIYGN CC+++CAPABLE OF EVERYTHING HE WAS CAPABLE+++GLYSD7TYBHFB
HNCMDKSL, IL OSJPKS 'OWOJUIG

+++LIED TO YOU BECAUSE I LIKED IT, I COULD PRETE+++B CX DSUH7T77567777 BFVV

+++GOOD OLD J.K!+++HBFSVH-DN-B63VBS S DD+++SAFE, SHE'S WITH HER FAMILY+++

VHKACSJAD N7T62--223NC+++LOVE TRAVELLING WITH YOU+++

KLIAHD;IA;;NNBD2UYERKUBK;'ZPFLBHV8Y78Y23VJHVKY BSWR26R3EGHVN
QEIOF+++DID YOU MISS ME?+++,JDFSKBEFDD

+++HELLO! OOH, NEW TEETH+++